Contents

Preface

Some of the subject matter of this book has been dealt with in previous publications of mine. I acknowledge these passages in footnotes as the text unfolds. What is essentially new to this work is the overall encapsulation of a period of time which has, I think, not been adequately considered. That is, the long ages when much of the rest of the country which became Britain was in a process of repeated distintegration and reconstruction, during which the bit which became recognised as Wales was all the time under the rule of succeeding generations of a single family, descendants of Rhodri Mawr, with credible claims to pedigrees much earlier than that, going back to Maelgwn Gwynedd and even Cunedda, to 400 AD, to the start of our recorded history.

It is this sort of continuity which defines Wales. Perhaps this basis for its awareness of its past underpins its resilience to the forces of change which have consistently beset it – as indeed they have all cultural identities – and gives it still the confidence to face the present, and, I am sure, the future.

Michael Senior
Glan Conwy, 2017

Continuity and resilience as defined in the landscape of Wales

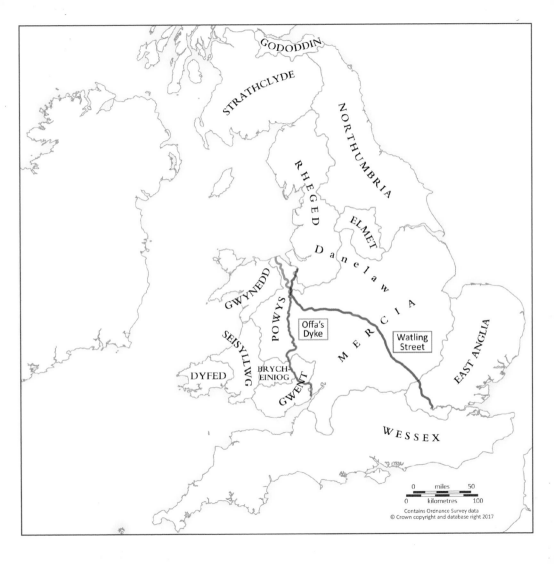

GODODDIN

STRATHCLYDE

NORTHUMBRIA

RHEGED

Danelaw

ELMET

GWYNEDD

POWYS

Offa's Dyke

MERCIA

Watling Street

EAST ANGLIA

SEISYLLWG

DYFED

BRYCH-EINIOG

GWENT

WESSEX

0   miles   50
0   kilometres   100

Contains Ordnance Survey data
© Crown copyright and database right 2017

This nation, O king, may now, as in former times, be harassed, and in a great measure weakened and destroyed by your and other powers, and it will often prevail by its laudable exertions; but it can never be totally subdued through the wrath of man, unless the wrath of God shall concur. Nor do I think, that any other nation than this of Wales, or any other language, whatever may hereafter come to pass, shall, in the day of severe examination before the Supreme Judge, answer for this corner of the earth.

So an old man said to a king.

Henry II of England might not have expected to get this answer, when, during his invasion of southern Wales, he asked an old Welsh supporter at Pencader in Carmarthenshire what his opinion was of the strength of the English army and the likely resistance of the Welsh, and the probable outcome of his invasion. The conversation is recorded for us by Gerald of Wales at the end of his *Description of Wales*, which he finished in 1194.[1]

Wales is so often defined by exclusion (in that it is not England) that it is heartening to find that at a crucial stage in the development of the idea it was a positive, assertive concept. This book sets out to define what it is, about this corner of the world, which makes it permanently definable as Wales. There has been from the start so much attrition from the outside world, and so much division within, that it should apparently have gone out of the conceptual system at once. The answer might lie somewhere in the four hundred years of the development of its identity – between the first near-unification in the time of Rhodri Mawr and the enforced capitulation to the Normans on the death of the last Llywelyn – which is the period to be dealt with here. It is perhaps worth noting that something must be gained in terms of identity by the fact that Wales held out against the Norman invaders two hundred and sixteen years longer than England did.

In this book we will trace the emergence of Wales as a geopolitical unit, and in the process see it overcoming the

Ceinau hen Gymro wrth Harri II, frenin Lloegr ym Mhencader yn 1163

Gellir gorthrymu'r genedl hon yn wir, ac i raddau helaeth iawn ei distrywio
ar llosgau trwy dy nerthoedd di, O frenin, ac eiddo eraill 'yn awr megis cynt
a llawer gwaith eto pan haedda hynny. Er deleu'n llwyr, fodd bynnag, trwy
ddigofaint dyn, ni ellir, onis bydd helyd ddigofaint Duw yn cydredeg ag ef.
Ac nid unrhyw genedl arall, fel y barnaf i, amgen na hon o'r Cymry, nac
unrhyw iaith arall, ar Ddydd y Farn ddostlem gerbron y Barnwr Goruchaf,
pa beth bynnag a ddigwyddo i'r amfeddill amuyaf ohoni, a fydd yn ateb
dros y gongl fach hon o'r ddaear.   Plaid Cymru a'i cododd 1952

The old Man of Pencader's memorial plaque

fragmentation which was the aftermath of its tribal origins. We will inevitably be confronted with the interaction with the parallel development of the English kingdoms, themselves feeling their way towards their own unification at the same time. At this crucial period, when for instance Hywel Dda attended the court councils of Athelstan of Wessex, did the flow of influence perhaps go both ways?

It becomes obvious in the process that the weaknesses and problems within the English kingdoms, once those had been established, gave opportunities to the newly unified Welsh. For much of this period there were times at which one or other group of Germanic invaders needed the help of the Welsh in support of their struggle against another faction of their own people. Alliances were built, we shall see, which had the potential to become national power-blocks; but we shall also see the essentially temporary character of early medieval politics. Those engaged in that struggle for survival could have done with the benefit of our hindsight. One group might then have seen the ghost of a future 'Greater Mercia', incorporating Wessex, leading towards the formulation of something which was (anyway, and later, and by hard-won incidence) to become the entity of England. Meanwhile the other group still fumbled with the aftermath of the decaying concepts of Gwynedd and Powys, among other kingdoms, and only gradually, in recognisable steps, managed to form of this the concept of Wales.

They got to that resolution in the end, of course. But it is tantalising for us to see that it might have been achieved with less anguish.

NOTES

1. **Gerald of Wales**: *Gerald de Barri (c. 1146–1223), frequently known as Giraldus Cambrensis, since he wrote in Latin. I use the text here, and will again later, of the Everyman edition of 1908 edited by W. Llewelyn Williams, which is the 1806 translation by Sir Richard Colt Hoare. I have not presumed to check or revise Hoare's translation from the Latin, largely because I admire his manner of Gerald's own church Latin. There is no suggestion that Gerald was present when the encounter described took place, which was probably on the occasion of Henry's incursion into southern Wales, so we must take the description of it to be possibly an invention by Gerald or his informants, but it well illustrates his assessment of the mood of Wales at the time.*

1. Gerald of Wales' statue in Cardiff;
2. Maenorbier castle – Gerald's birthplace

Rhodri Mawr

In 843 the Frankish empire which had been amassed by Charlemagne officially fell apart.

Charlemagne had died in 814, and the lands he had integrated became controlled by his youngest son Louis (the others having predeceased him), an arrangement which was only strong enough to last for one generation. By the treaty of Verdun, in 843, the vast territories including what is now Germany, France and Italy were split between three of Charlemagne's grandsons. It was the end of something, and the beginning. It was the final flourish of disintegration of the great Roman empire, saved for a time by the establishment, under the Pope, of its successor, the Holy Roman Empire. From then on Europe was to be a loose amalgamation of nation states – Burgundy, Flanders, Aquitaine, Lorraine – with a weakening centralising force, the emperor in Vienna, struggling to be heard.

It is all the more surprising, given this historical genesis, to find that in Wales rather the reverse was happening. In 844, a year after the Verdun treaty, Rhodri, the son of Merfyn Frych, king of Gwynedd, and his wife Nest, daughter of a king of Powys, inherited the kingdom of Gwynedd. Eleven years later, on the death of his mother's brother, he inherited the kingdom of Powys too. Since he married the daughter of a king of Seisyllwg he inherited that kingdom also, in 871, when his wife's brother died. The unification of these formerly competing kingdoms was of great importance to Rhodri and to Wales, since had they been (as they usually were) at each other's throats neither of them could have resisted the onslaught of attack which Rhodri then experienced, from Mercia, from Wessex, and from Denmark.

Although this prominent position seems to have come to him from good fortune rather than intention it then becomes plain that it could not have happened to a more suitable man. Nor was it, actually, entirely unplanned. The Welsh system of inheritance (which we shall encounter again in this book) favoured division over primogeniture, a system

Maen Gwynedd – 'Gwynedd's stone' showing the path to Bwlch Maen Gwynedd on the border of Gwynedd and Powys

which led throughout society, from the greatest kingdom to the smallest farm, to increasingly weak and unviable units. Although it seems it could not be overtly broken (presumably because of the surge of resentment that would cause) for practical reasons its weaknesses had to be, wherever possible, overcome. The compensation, favoured both by great kings and by judicious farmers, was advantagious marriage.

We have seen this (already in this so-far brief story) take place in Rhodri's case twice. His father, king of Gwynedd, had married his mother, heiress of Powys. He himself married the heiress of Seisyllwg. The throne in both cases passed to the brothers of the heiress, but then to her son in one case and her husband in the other.[1]

Rhodri was about twenty-four when he became king of Gwynedd, and within ten years the demands of his position had begun to make themselves apparent. When he inherited Powys a new unity was created between the two main dynasties of northern and central Wales. Eastern Powys had fallen to Mercia in 822, and Mercia shortly after, in 828, itself fell to Wessex. Egbert of Wessex, who had ruled for nearly thirty-eight years, died in 839 and left an unsettled inheritance in which his two sons divided between them the powerful kingdom he had ruled. Egbert had viewed the Welsh neighbouring kingdoms with ambivalence, since he needed the backing of Wales against a probable Mercian uprising. On the other hand when Rhodri claimed his inherited kingdom the heirs of Wessex were not prepared simply to hand it over. It was in this situation that Rhodri found himself, as king of two main provinces, under threat from two sides. As king of Powys he had to keep a wary eye on Wessex. As king of Gwynedd he found himself seriously threatened from the sea.

The Welsh chronicles call them Kenedloed, which means (now spelt Cenhedloedd) 'Gentiles' or more often Kenedloed Duon, 'Black Gentiles'.[2] The Annals, which call them more specifically by the borrowed word Nordmanieit, 'Norsemen', inform us that they had arrived in southern Ireland in 796, and the chronicles add that they ravaged Anglesey in 855, sacked York in 867, and destroyed Dunbarton in 871. Later known as Danes, these invaders had become an organised force by Rhodri's reign, and are perhaps to be distinguished from the Norwegian raiders along the Welsh coast.

We know them all now as Vikings. The word comes from a Scandinavian term 'vik', meaning a cove or bay. It was used, in the Anglo-Saxon form wicing, to describe pirates in general. The association, particularly in the Welsh texts, with paganism, leading to the use of the word Gentile, was emphasised by the fact that the Scandinavians had no qualms about plundering monasteries and churches.

Rhodri defeated them in Anglesey (which island they had overrun in 853), in a significant battle in 856, but it did not benefit him for long. By the 870s Mercia was seeking to expand, and the only way it could do so was by invading Wales.

The reason for this is that by then the whole of Mercia east of Watling Street was in Danish hands. Once the Vikings had started to settle, rather than just raid, they had to be dealt with diplomatically as well as in battle. A crucial entry in the Anglo-Saxon Chronicles for the year 876 signals a step change in that direction. Using here the approximation of modern script, it reads:

... thy geare Healfdene Northanhymbra long gedelde ergende waeron hiera tilgende.

Anne Savage's translation, in the Book Club Associates' edition of The Anglo-Saxon Chronicles is simple and straightforward:

> That year Healfdene shared out Northumbrian land, and they were ploughing and providing for themselves.

A perhaps slightly more stringently academic version provided by the Rev. James Ingram in 1823 is more literal but also more obscure:

> The same year Healfden divided the land of the Northumbrians; so that they became afterwards their harrowers and plowers.

They were farming. They had made the crucial move from the hunting activity of summer raids to the way of life which involves, and enables, settlement. No doubt many of the seafarers had been engaged in farming as well as fishing in their homeland. But there the land was poor and the climate hard, at least in comparison to the rich soils of Wessex and Mercia. With this news we look both backwards and forwards, in this story. We see in their new activity the reason they had come, population increase having led to territorial conflict on the farmlands, mainly steep sheep-pastures, of Denmark and Norway. We aslo see in it the situation which was about to develop.

Because they were looking for fruitful land, and their access to it from the sea was up the larger navigable rivers, Wales did not greatly interest the new settlers. On the whole neither requirement applied here. Rhodri felt their influence largely at second hand, through their pressure on his neighbours, Mercia and Wessex. The one exception to this condition was Anglesey, where flat and fertile land adjoining the sea was tempting to them.

As mentioned, the Norsemen had invaded Anglesey in 853. Although there is no evidence of this they may have settled, and so perhaps expanded in number, which would explain why Rhodri decided to confront them there in 856.[3] The fact that he defeated them, and killed their leader Horm (or Gorm), seems to have settled the matter for the time being, and it was not in the end to be Vikings, but Mercians, who would bring about the end of Rhodri's reign.

In due course the situation which had developed during the 860s and 870s was formalised by a Treaty between Alfred and the Danish leader Guthrum in 886, and we may regard what is set out then as being the situation arrived at in the decades before. Using the ancient highway, Watling Street, as a western border, it agreed that if the Danes had their own territory to the east of it they would leave the Mercians to the west unmolested. Thus was formed the territory known as the 'Danelaw', which extended up the west coast as far as Strathclyde, and on the east coast as far as the border with Northumberland. Watling Street, now largely the A5, running through the middle of Mercia, is a natural division between the west and eastern Midlands.

The relationship of Mercia and Wales was mainly warily co-operative during

A Viking skeleton (1) and Viking artefacts (2) found during archaeological work at Llanbedr-goch, Anglesey (3)

Rhodri's time. Offa's Dyke had for nearly a hundred years worked both ways, keeping the Welsh from stealing Mercian cattle while protecting the most fruitful lands in northern Wales from Mercian exploitation. Rhodri's victory over the Danes in Anglesey in 856 did a big favour to the Mercians, and indeed also to the West Saxons. It is ironic that although much of Rhodri's military activity was against the Danes, his final battle was an attempt to turn the Mercians, this time, out of Anglesey.

The chronicles do not give much information about the battle, just that Rhodri and his brother Gwriad were slain by the Saxons, *gan y Saeson*, in 878.[4] We know that the term is being used as a generalisation; it was not the West Saxons Rhodri had to deal with, since Alfred was a long way away fighting the Vikings in eastern England, and then being defeated by them in Somerset, at the time.

Mercia had largely come to share its history with Wessex during this time, the years after Rhodri succeeded to the throne of Gwynedd. Both kingdoms were preoccupied with the Viking threats, though in different ways. Mercia was still under pressure from the east, where the Danes who were centred on York pressed its borders; it seems probable that the attempted resolution in the form of the Danelaw treaty was not taken entirely seriously by either side, and the competition for good land (which also affected Wales) continued. Wessex on the other hand had to resist Danish invasions on its southern coast. The Danes overwintered in Britain in 851, sacked Canterbury, rebuffed the Mercians, but, in a sign of changing fortunes, were resoundingly defeated by the men of Wessex.

Though the rise in power of Wessex during this period is inseparable from the ability and personality of Alfred, who became king only in the last phase of Rhodri's reign in Wales, the ambitions of the kingdom had been clear from Egbert onwards, and did not end, indeed, with Alfred. Having absorbed Mercia in its weakened state, and weakened it further with the institution of the Danelaw, Wesex then turned its attention to Northumbria. It took in fact five generations of substantial kings to unify England. Alfred

1. Offa's Dyke near Cefn Llanfair; 2. near Hawthorn Hill; 3. from the air

was in the middle of this chain: grandson of Egbert, grandfather of Athelstan.

The transformation of Wales from a number of individual kingdoms into three is highlighted by John Davies, in his definitive book, *A History of Wales*.[5] Davies points out, usefully, that the process by which this came about is impossible to reconcile 'with the notion that the territory of a Welsh king was divided after his death among all his sons.' From the time of Maelgwn in the sixth century to the reign of Rhodri was 'about a dozen generations'. If each king in the line is imagined to have had two sons (a modest hypothesis, he points out) and every one of them had received part of Maelgwn's original kingdom, 'by the age of Rhodri there would have been 2,048 kings in Gwynedd', rulers, if they were lucky, of kingdoms the size of smallholdings. 'Such foolishness is implicit in the idea that the Welsh had no concept of the unity of a kingdom, and that they lacked the political instinct which characterized others of the nations of Europe.' There was nothing, he observes, particularly unusual about the succession of kingship in early Wales. There was in Europe no cast-iron rule for determining who was the king's heir. It was a matter of who was the strongest and most able.

There were other factors conducive to the amalgamation of power. There was at the time – the time of Rhodri and Alfred – a powerful impetus to see a country's identity as being founded on its cohesive history. We find this evidenced in the fact that both those kings encouraged the writing of material dealing with a continuous succession from a time of primal blissful self-identity.

The Welsh Annals record events from the year 447, and continue with brief ecclesiastical notices (the death of bishops, the movements of missionary saints) noting the two exploits of Arthur, at Badon and Camlan, the death of Maelgwn Gwynedd and the battle of Arfderydd. It is thought that they were compiled in chronicle form from about 954, but their origins as clerical documents makes it likely that the references within them were actualy originally made in the year to which they refer.

Dinas Emrys – King Gwrtheyrn fled from his London court to this stronghold in Snowdonia as the Germanic tribes invaded Britain from the east

Meanwhile the Anglo-Saxon Chronicle starts its records much earlier, dealing with matters of the Roman empire and early years of Christianity, until with the period of the fifth century we come to its titular subject, and the formation of the Anglo-Saxon kingdoms. Then in the year 495 we are told that an ealdorman called Cerdic and his son Cynric came to Britain (it is not said where from) with five ships, and on the same day fought the Welsh. The royal line of Wessex, it is implied, was founded by them.

The writing, copying and distributing of the Chronicle is agreed to be due to the enthusiasm of Alfred. The king himself says of the period before his reign that there were happy times then throughout England, and gives his reason for translating texts into English as the decline of the knowledge of Latin during his century. Once there had been wisdom and learning in Wessex, such that 'people from abroad' came there for instruction; now if we wished for knowledge we should have to seek it outside. There were very

The site of an early Christian church at Llanfaglan near Caernarfon

few men on this side of the Humber now 'who could translate a single letter from Latin into English... There were so few of them that I cannot recollect even a single one south of the Thames when I succeeded to the kingdom.' Thus while the Welsh Annals were still produced in Latin, and continued to be so, the Anglo-Saxon Chronicle was (unusually for European history) produced in the vernacular. So, as we shall see, was much other literature. Alfred wanted his people educated, and he faced the fact that unless works were produced in English they could not be read.

Alfred saying that the people of Wessex in his time had to seek instruction from outside speaks for himself, and his opinion is proved by his deeds. In about 880 he poached the cleric Asser from St David's. 'I was summoned by the king from the remote, westernmost parts of Wales...' Alfred had a habit of attracting other people's intellectuals to his court: he borrowed Grimbald from Flanders, and John the Old Saxon from eastern Francia. But making Asser into a member of his household and finally his biographer is a significant move from our present point of view. It is evidence that at least in this case influence went from Wales to Wessex, not the reverse.

Meanwhile in Wales Rhodri's court fostered the creation of a whole body of literature which celebrated the golden past of his ancestors, the time when Wales and northern Britain were still united, an idealised heroic age illuminated by the concept of the 'Men of the North'. Among these was Llywarch Hen, a sixth century prince from whom Rhodri was supposed to be descended.

Though there undoubtedly was such a person, the body of literature which got attached to him three hundred years later is more impelled by the state of Powys when Rhodri ruled over it than by anything which can have been known about Llywarch's actual time. According to the pedigrees Llywarch was a cousin of the king of Rheged, a northern British kingdom, and so a figure of the 'Old North' (*Yr Hen Ogledd*)[6] and in contention with Ida of Northumbria, much as Rhodri was with Alfred of Wessex. It was however a competent bard (or bards) of Rhodri's Powys who reinvented Llywarch as the central character in a saga of stories now set firmly in eastern Powys.

These take the form of a series of poems, written in the style known as the *englyn*. This is a strict verse form, perhaps used here for the first time, involving a set pattern of numbers of syllables, in which (among other specifications) one syllable sets the rhymes for subsequent lines. In spite of its patently complex formal structure the result can often seem quite simple, and the constraints of the tradition can give to the language a tension and force which a more free-flowing verse form might have lacked.

Powys, in the Llywarch poems, is a disaster zone. The mood of the works gives us some insight into the state of the kingdom when Rhodri took it over. The poems are thought to be all that is left of a long prose saga, the rest being lost, in which these 'songs' are monologue or dialogue breaks in the narrative sequence. Central to the corpus are, for instance, the song of an old man, *Can yr henwr*, a mourning for lost times and lament on age spoken by Llywarch himself; and *Canu Heledd*, a series of laments supposedly spoken by the sister of Cynddylan, a lord

The ford on Morlas brook (the present day Wales/England border) which features in the Llywarch poems

of Powys based in Pengwern (now Shrewsbury) in the early seventh century. The poems are dated by Sir Ifor Williams to about 850, and so are using the distant past of the same area to mourn the state of Powys in Rhodri's time.[7]

The former poem is of the three-line *englyn* throughout. For instance (in Anthony Conran's translation, in the *Penguin Book of Welsh Verse*):

Ere my back was bent, I was bold,
Was welcomed in the beer-hall
Of Powys, paradise of Welshmen.

The poem is a long one; Llywarch regrets his loss of mobility, reduced to a world governed by his crutch, mocked by old age. His sons are dead, a theme enlarged on in the other prominent poem of the cycle.

Canu Heledd, Heledd's song, is set in the same context as the Llywarch cycle; Heledd's brothers, like Llywarch's sons, have all been killed, leaving her as the last surviving representative of the old royal line of Powys. Just as Llywarch mourned his last son Gwen, so Heledd regrets the loss of Cynddylan, her brother. *Stafell Gynddylan*, Cynddylan's Hall, is particularly poignant.

Every one of its sixteen three-line *englynion* begins with the line 'Cynddylan's hall is dark tonight' (*Stafell Gynddylan, ys tywyll heno*, in the original old-Welsh form), or a variant of it.

Quiet is Cynddylan's hall tonight
Now it has lost its lord.
Merciful God, what shall I do?

The process which we see going on here is sometimes referred to as a renaissance, being the appeal to a memory of a lost kingdom, and this condition of harking back to a golden age is characteristic also of the surrounding literature of this richly fruitful time. Because of this impulse to revivalism, the court poets of the kingdoms of the north, such as those of Rheged and Gododdin, have enjoyed two separate entries into history, that of their origins in the heroic world of the sixth century, and that of their rediscovery and to a large extent reinvention, in the idealised construct of the heroic age as envisaged at another court, that of Rhodri in the ninth.

1. Penmon priory; 2. An early Christian cross at Penmon 3. Ffynnon Seiriol – the saint's well

Aneirin, for instance, who is named along with Taliesin by Nennius, writing in probably 829, as being 'famous in British verse', was almost certainly a late sixth century poet who wrote at Edinburgh, when Welsh was still the language of southern Scotland. Though it is available to us now only in a thirteenth century manuscript, the *Llyfr Aneirin*, Sir Ifor Williams has shown by textual analysis that most of *Y Gododdin*, the great epic poem attributed to Aneirin, dates from the sixth century, and interpolations belong to the period of its revival, the ninth century, and the cultural tradition of recalling the world of the Old North which flourished then, in the reign of Rhodri Mawr.

Of the same provenance are the works of Taliesin, two groups of which are closely associated with the poet himself (as opposed to being recognsiably additions likely to have been made by later scribes): historical poems which may have been his work and so of his time, the sixth century, dealing mainly with the exploits of Urien, king of Rheged, praise of him, his death and succession by his son Owain; and a group which Sir Ifor Williams thought belonged to a Taliesin cult of perhaps the ninth century, the age of Rhodri.

Much the same could be said of Myrddin, another probably factual sixth century poet, who became later saddled with mystical prophecies in the eleventh and twelfth centuries and ended immortally as the wizard Merlin. In terms of imagery the mythic figures made of both Taliesin and Myrddin are interesting as nostalalic throwbacks to the composite role of druid and bard. By the ninth century, these poets were connected to places in the current Welsh kingdoms.

In wishing to record and promote their people's history, and in the process to remember a great and ancient past for the same group of people, and a cultural heritage of some wealth, both Rhodri in Wales and Alfred in Wessex were, at the same time, repeating something which had shortly before been done by Charlemagne, whether they knew this or not. The so-called Carolingian Renaissance lasted a relatively short time – from the late eighth century until the ninth – but it set a structure for later European education. Charlemagne had attracted to his court

The cromlech known as 'Bedd Taliesin' above Cors Fochno, the location of another Taliesin legend and the Dyfi estuary

prominent scholars from several other countries, notable among them Alcuin of York, who became leader of the Palace School. These formal scholarly groups had an agenda consisting of several themes. They sought to recover the level of culture of the late Roman empire, and to cultivate literacy in Latin, which had been falling out of use in the Frankish zones just as it had in Alfred's Wessex, though not apparently in Wales. A sort of enlightenment was fostered by an emphasis on the application of reason, and by a general enthusiasm for knowledge. Alfred's desire that his countrymen should be educated and should have the literature of their antecedants made available to them, and Rhodri's evident favouring of the same principles, seem like echoes of this.

Rather than trying to trace lines of influence perhaps we should be looking for a common cause, and wonder what it was that set several centres of civilisation on the same route to self-rediscovery at more or less the same time. The impulse to value localised unity and to legitimise it by reference to history is one which occurs in continents from time to time, and it is reasonable to see it as the response to the removal of the centralising constraint of an imposed power: in this case a re-emerging of ancient nationalism when the geat Roman Empire finally collapsed.

1. **Welsh inheritance customs.** *Doubt is sometimes cast on the claim that Rhodri could have inherited territory in this way, since Welsh custom did not recognise inheritance through the maternal line. It is suggested that instead his acquisition of the rule of Powys and then Seisyllwg was brought about by foul-play on his part, and the suppositiion that he gained them through his mother and then his wife was propaganda concocted on his behalf. This is of course quite possible, but the tradition of his rightful status is sufficiently strong for us to concur with it, albeit recognising the doubt.*

2. **Gentiles.** *Alternatively translated as 'heathen or pagan', since 'gentile' also carries the meaning of 'belonging to an alien religion'. The word probably comes from the Latin, gentilis, which means a clansman, a person of a single 'gens', that is a people, tribe or nation.*

3. **Vikings in Anglesey.** *Some apparent cultural influence on artefacts such as the stone cross at Penmon, and a Viking burial found at Benllech, indicate the possibility of settlement, and certainly the many Viking place-names along the coast of Wales provide proof of regular and long-term familiarity with this region, but the only archaeological evidence for any establshed Viking settlement (so far) is at Llanbedrgoch, where an apparent trading post was discovered in 1994 near Aberllleiniog castle, though its period of occupation is given as the tenth century.*

4. **The death of Rhodri.** *There are variants of the record of this event. The Annals of Wales has the date as 877, 878 being the date given in the Chronicles of the Princes. The Annals also say that Gwriad was his son, not brother.*

5. **John Davies.** A History of Wales. Allen Lane. The Penguin Press. English edition 1993. Pp. 95-6.

6. **The Old North.** *Before the expansion of Northumbria in the early ninth century the north of what is now England, together with southern Scotland, was politically and linguistically joined to the area which became Wales; this northern confederation consisted of the tribal kingdoms of Gododdin, Rheged, Strathclyde and Elmet. Early medieval Welsh literature looks back on this time with evident pride, as a heroic period, the 'Men of the North', Gwyr y Gogledd, being portrayed as anestral to the reigning dynasties of the Welsh, and the culture tracing its roots to the warrior-poets of that iconic world.*

7. **Sir Ifor Williams.** *(1881–1965) Editing early Welsh poetry was his life's work. Head of the Welsh Department at Bangor University from 1920 until his retirement in 1947; his books, lectures and radio talks form a large part of the present understanding of the status of early Welsh literature. Sir Ifor's dating of the composition of the prose cycles in which the poems were thought to be embedded is accepted at about 850, which place them in the context of the peaceful union of Gwynedd and Powys brought about by the marriage of Rhodri's parents. Some recent academics suggest that they were composed to celebrate that peace, perhaps by a bard of Gwynedd. In any case the result of importing heroes from a distant time in the lost lands of the north into a thriving (though threatened) Wales was to give Welsh literature the impetus for a major revival.*

See also: The Penguin Book of Welsh Verse, *translated and introduced by Anthony Conran, Penguin Books Ltd. 1967; and* An Introduction to Welsh Poetry, *Gwyn Williams, Faber, 1953. pp. 18-70.*

Hywel Dda

When Rhodri died there was no immediate single successor to his power. He had several sons (some say six), of whom two became prominent. The eldest, Anarawd, became king of Gwynedd, and as such the founder of a dynasty (the House of Aberffraw) which ended with the two Llywelyns. He it was who decisively checked Mercian ambitions of extension westwards, at the battle fought on the west bank of the Conwy river in 880, *Dial Rodri*, in which God (and Anarawd) avenged Rhodri, or so the *Brut y Tywysogyon* tells us.[1] Meanwhile the second son Cadell was allocated the kingdom of Seisyllwg, composed of Ceredigion and Ystrad Tywi, and his brother Merfyn that of Powys. Cadell, it seems, adjusted this situation by killing Merfyn and absorbing Powys, thus forming the core of a considerable kingdom which became known as Deheubarth. Hywel, known subsequently as Hywel the Good, Hywel Dda, was Cadell's son.

The division of Rhodri's considerable territory, which seemed to be following the old Welsh custom of partible inheritance, evidently could not survive for long against the prevailing drive, during the ninth century, towards unification. Although Cadell had left Seisyllwg in two halves to his two sons, Hywel's brother Clydog died in 920 with the result that he took over the whole, and when Hywel married the daughter of the king of Dyfed the possession of that kingdom came to him as well. There remained Gwynedd, ruled by Idwal, son of Anarawd, though nominally at least subject to the overlordship, at this time, of Wessex. Idwal led a revolt against the Saxons in 942, in which he was killed, and although he had two sons who expected to inherit these were expelled, and his cousin Hywel took over Gwynedd and Powys. He thus ruled all Wales, except the smaller south-east kingdoms of Morgannwg and Gwent.

This account of this rather murky period is inevitably simplistic. Much disentangling is needed of the records of possible facts from their overlay of

Aberffraw, Anglesey: the seat of the kings of Gwynedd

Alfred's statue at Winchester

expediency on his part, but he may also have had help or encouragement from the king of Wessex. In the light of later developments it is tempting to see that it would be to Wessex's advantage to have Gwynedd and Powys ruled by a puppet king.

We do at least know that by the time Hywel got to rule over almost the whole of Wales he had firmly cemented alliances with the dominant English kingdom. As early as 918 he went with his brother and Idwal of Gwynedd to do homage to Alfred's son Edward, and about 936 he and Owain of Gwent submitted to Edward's son Athelstan at Hereford. It is sometimes said that many of his deeds and characteristics show the influence of Alfred, and quite possibly this inclination also lay behind his decision to make the pilgrimage to Rome, which he did in 928. Alfred had done this twice, once as a child in 853 and again together with his father, in 855. Hywel's decision to seek peace whenever possible with his powerful neighbours may well have been mainly realistic: perhaps he could see that there was no alternative, and that his own ends might be best served by accepting that fact. But it is certainly also possible to argue that he had a personal predilection

dynastic propaganda. Can Hywel really have been given the kingdom of Dyfed as a result of marrying the daughter of its king? Was he perhaps in possession of much of it already? At this early stage the thought arises: just how Good was Hywel? The forced exile of Idwal's sons from Gwynedd may have been a simple act of for the same cultural values as did the house of Alfred.

There is, anyway, ample evidence that he spent more time at the court of Athelstan than one would expect. John Davies points out that beside appearing in lists of client kings in attendance he is cited as a witness to English royal charters on seven occasions. That means, I think, that he was frequently there. This personal disposal had a profound effect on the history of both countries.

It also probably influenced the production of the matter for which he is best known, the 'Laws', *Cyfraith Hywel*. Once again it is possible to see a cultural trend stemming from Charlemagne through Alfred, for producing national bodies of literature which served to identify and unify their respective peoples. But Hywel's Laws have more significance, than that of being a product of their time. Examination of the text proves the existence of a long-built-up body of social code stretching back some centuries before the time of Hywel; and this forms the foundation for the future of the national cohesion which is the essence of the emerging country of Wales. As John Davies succinctly puts it: 'The Law is among the most splendid creations of the culture of the Welsh.'

On the face of it we should have no doubt about how this happened, because it is set out clearly in the Prologue. In Dafydd Jenkins's translation:

> Hywel son of Cadell prince of all Wales saw the Welsh misusing the laws and called to him six men from every cantred in Wales, to the White House on Taf. These were to be the wisest men in the realm, four of them laymen and the other two clerks. This was the reason for bringing the clerks: lest the laymen should set down anything which might be against Holy Scripture.[2]

The White House, it seems to be established, is a reference to the present town of Whitland, Carmarthenshire, which lies fifteen miles west of Carmarthen, mid-way between Narberth and St. Clears. Its name in Welsh is Hendygwyn, 'old white house', which may have derived originally from the Cistercian abbey which once stood nearby – white being the characterising colour of the monks' habits. The laymen and clerks

referred to are seen as lawyers and clerics.

The only trouble with this apparently detailed factual description is that it is now held to be highly doubtful. The meeting at Whitland almost certainly never took place. The give-away is that as the copies of the Law developed the Prologue became more assertive, and it seems likely that it was felt necessary to enhance it, and to locate the initiation of the codification of tradition at a certain place and time, to counter the criticism that the laws are based on pagan tradition, which would incur the hostility of the Church.

There are some aspects of the production of the Laws which are clear enough, and other points on which expert opinion is agreed. We have the text now in forty-two different manuscripts of diffrerent dates, ranging from the early thirteenth to the early sixteenth centuries, during which period these books were still in practical use in courts of law. The copies we have were therefore, at one time, lawyers' hand books. This does not mean that all that they contain was relevant at

Rhosyr, Anglesey – one of the courts of the Gwynedd kings

the time they were transcribed, since old and outdated law was retained as a record, and new law added. This means, it is often remarked, that we cannot identify from the texts of the Law anything certain about the customs or conditions of the time at which the manuscript of that text was written. It is only assumed that when (or if) Hywel called together representative lawyers and clerics, in about 930 AD, it was to modify and clarify a body of work which was already in existence.

The tendency to accept this point – that some at least of the Law as retained in later years was already ancient – is encouraged by the fact that it would have made sense. Hywel had good reasons for a decision to gather and codify the legal customs of his people. He had recently occupied several quite diverse territories, each presumably with their own ancient habits of administration. He had, as king over what were previously different places, a reasonable impulse to seek unification, standardisation, centralisation. This consideration gives us at least an inclination to believe that Hywel was personally involved in what became the *Cyfraith Hywel*, or (since six of the early manuscripts are in Latin) the *Lex Hoeli*.

The King in the law manuscript

It is, then, wise to bear in mind the qualification we have just made: that because the Law was constantly evolving, during its period of use, yet also retaining, like embedded fossils, items from its long history, we cannot read it as a record of its time. Nevertheless there are some remarkable characteristics of attitude and principle apparent from its pages which mark it out as being different from the laws of other kingdoms, and from the laws which succeeded it in Wales after Unification. These features certainly tell us something about the ethos of medieval Wales.

It is true, first, that even if the laws were instituted by a king, they remain folk law, not state law, since they arise from the need to deal with everyday local and personal matters, rather than matters of duty and rights in relation to a higher authority. There are, certainly, passages, particularly at the start of all the vaious editions, where a hierarchy of sorts is set out, but with a mixed heroic and rustic flavour: the heir apparent, for instance, ('It is right for him to be a son or a nephew of the king') has a place in the court 'between the host and the chief falconer, as one of the six men of the King's mess'. He lodges with his pages 'and the fueller to light a fire and shut the doors'. The placing of all the officers of the court is elaborately set out, the priest, the chaired bard, the chief groom, the chief huntsman, as these inheritors of a travelling warband all dine together in the Great Hall. Elsewhere it has been noted, from the point of view of legal history, that compensation is a common aim rather than punishment, the latter penalty becoming tentatively apparent as the state became a stronger force.

1. and 2. Different law sections, Cyfraith Hywel

After a long section detailing the behaviour of the court, we are surprised to find the Law opening with a chapter devoted to the laws of women, and more so that this deals first with disposal of property on separation. Husband and wife have both farmyard and domestic goods to share: pigs, sheep, goats, milk vessels, a riddle (his) and a fine sieve (hers). In the bedroom, she gets the top sheet, he the bottom one. Out in the yard and the field she takes the broad axe, the hedging bill and the ploughshare; his share is the barn and the crops, and all the hens. The cats are hers, all except one – he gets to keep one of the cats. Hardly surprisingly they each keep their own clothes, 'except their mantels' which are shared. The long and detailed specification of rights in separation settlement paints a picture of a simple and basic rural world, but one in which women have established and comparable status.

Status is, in fact, a matter of concern to the law-writers, and an elaborate class system becomes apparent. This is based partly on the distinction of the bonded and the free, a system thought to be originally derived from the conquest of a former population in perhaps pre-historic times, in which the invaded natives were allowed to remain on their land but deprived of certain rights. By the early Middle Ages this class of society (that of the *aillt*, plural *eilltion*) were the descendants of the people who farmed the Prince's land rather than their own, so that although they were in bond it was not to the free farmers but to the state. There is no doubt, from Hywel's Law, that their status was regarded as inferior. The class of free property holders was called the *uchelwyr*, a level of the hierarchy which developed into the squirearchy in later times. Administration was overseen by officers known as the *maer* and the *cyngellor*, not, apparently, directly translatable as mayor and chancellor, but having similar roles.

Land tenure was based on the unit of an acre, sixty-four of which made a holding. Four holdings amounted to a townland, and four townlands make a *maenol*, or, in some areas, *maenor*, a similar unit to our manor. This (Jenkins points out) is a highly schematic view of things in the Law, and the reality on the ground is much more varied.

Much of this is sensible and straightforward, but we are sometimes given sharp and shocking insights into a way of life of much more starkness and less sophistication than we would expect of the central Middle Ages. The law on rape, for instance, has the accuser being put through a quasi-religious ritual, so bizarre that we cannot believe that it was ever taken seriouly, unless it were simply a way of saying that it is not expected that accusations of rape will ever be brought to court.[3]

The details of what people can and cannot do, or should and should not, give us a sharp and often surprising view of the predicaments, and the crises, which they face, as they go about their daily domestic lives in a world which is so clearly unlike ours but is evidently very real to them. Most obviously they live in a rural context, in which it makes sense to see things in terms of practical reality. If you fell a tree, and it kills somebody, you are liable to compensation if you didn't warn them, but not if you did. If somebody who has caught rabies bites somebody else, who then dies, they are not liable for compensation for the death, because it was the disease which killed him, not the biter.

Land-law occupies much of the rest of the central book, disputes of ownership, damage to crops, and (again) the rights of women. We also get an insight into the business of royal administration, since this involves the impact of the mobile court on the King's representatives in the countryside.

To generalise, Wales is seen to be an essentially rural place. There were no towns, as John Davies says, 'for five hundred years or more'. We know that the few towns which had developled around the Roman camps had fallen out of use, with the deterioration of the Roman roads and a reversion to a subsistence agrarian way of life in place of a trading one, during the dark period of the seventh and eighth centuries. Farming was mixed, during whatever period we may choose as being represented by the Law: crops are to be protected from animals, each type of which is given a monetary value: horses, cattle, pigs, poultry, cats, dogs, hawks and bees. The ownership of cattle is seen to be sometimes at conflict with the growth of crops. Crops and hay-meadows are vulnerable to damage from livestock, and owners of animals have to keep them off another man's crop-land, or risk getting them impounded. Pigs are the most serious of the possible invaders, 'because they damage the land'. Judging by the detail it is felt necessary to specify, it seems that straying livestock causing damage to crops was a constant problem, in spite of the fact that both fences and hedges were in use to avoid this. Although matters of ownership, rights and inheritance are local, and strictly kin-based, as is compensation, the social group was mobile (practising transhumance), as was the constantly touring court. There

A judge

was recognition, even in this supposed codification, of regional differences. Women, for instance, are not entitled to patrimony, 'According to the men of Gwynedd'; and 'an innate man of Powys is not entitled to mother-right in Gwynedd, nor one of Gwynedd in Powys and also for Deheubarth'.

Whatever part, or lack of it, Hywel played in the formulation of the Law, it is for ever now associated with his name. This is in some ways unfair, since it masks the true role of a real and no doubt complex person. Hywel Dda in history played a part in a decisive period, with crucial consequences both for England and for Wales.

There is some doubt about whether this position was due to his diplomacy or to Athelstan's. There are indications that the latter was in a more powerful position. In 927, for instance, Athelstan took over the kingdom of Northumbria, and followed this by a treaty with all the remaining kings, 'first' (says the Anglo-Saxon Chronicle) 'Hywel, king of the West Welsh'. Together with Constantine, king of the Scots, and Owain, king of Gwent, they 'fastened a peace' at a place called Eamont Bridge (just south of Penrith, in Cumbria)

on July 12th, 'with pledges and oaths' and from there 'turned away in peace'. We may read between the lines that Hywel and Constantine and others did not have a lot of choice; but between 928 and 935 the Scots and the North British became increasingly restive, and it then made a lot of sense for Athelstan to keep Hywel on side. It was during this period that he appeared quite frequently at the English court. Athelstan's power, however, led to an inevitable reaction, and toward the end of the 930s Hywel must have wondered if he was on the right side.

The peace, however, while it lasted, gave both emerging nations, Wales and England, a chance to gather themselves into some sort of structure which they would not have had if they had remained at loggerheads. The temptation must have been apparent to both to remain in competition, for each to try to ensure that it was one of them, without the other, which would have achieved dominance over Britain. If Hywel recognised that Wales could not be itself without allowing England also the goal of self-recognition, his decision then enabled the glory of the

The Hywel Dda memorial garden at Whitland

next three hundred years. He could not, reasonably, have foreseen at that moment what would eventually happen. That is, he could not have anticipated the arrival of the Normans, nor prophesied the occurrence of an unusual antagonist. He could not have anticipated Edward I.

Nevertheless there are signs that in adopting a policy of appeasement towards Wessex Hywel found himself, at least temporarily, going against the tide of history. Some evidence of this is that about this time – 930s – there was written what John Davies calls 'one of the most remarkable of Welsh poems': *Armes Prydein*, The Prophecy of Britain. Since it seems that this literary work anticipated the anti-Athelstan alliance which then took place, it must be seen to reflect a power-group which was then in the making.

The *Armes Prydein* is a long poem, nearly two hundred lines, and is written in a relentless rhyme scheme in which a single rhyme is sustained for whole stanzas, sometimes as many as twenty lines at a time. This may give a certain opaque density to the sense of the poem, but the motivating bitterness is clear enough. It is a demand for action. The English had imposed a punitive tax on Wales, and now all the non-English peoples of Britain will join together to expel them from the island:

achymot kymry agwyr dulyn
Gwyddyl iwerdon mon aphrydyn
cornyw achludwys eu kynnwys genhyn

'There will be a coming-to-terms between the Welsh and the men of Dublin [the Viking colonists]; and the Irish of Ireland, men of Anglesey, the Picts, the Cornish,

and the northmen of Strathclyde'. In other words it was to be not just a Brythonic union, but an alliance of all non-Saxons involved in occupying Britain. Moreover the climactic confrontation was to be a resounding victory, dispelling the hated invaders for ever.

This is strange, if Sir Ifor Williams's painstaking dating of the poem, at about 930, is correct, because some seven years later exactly such a union of disparate forces took place, and the result was a catastrophic failure.

The Battle of Brunaburh is often hailed as one of the most important battles held on British soil, and it was early recognised as the largest battle which had taken place before the crucial encounter at Hastings. The importance of it was recognised at the time, and by both sides. In 927 Athelstan overcame the Vikings of York, and this brought about a situation in which Britain could remain temporarily at peace. It seems that in 934 a breach of the treaty by Constantine king of the Scots caused Athelstan to reassert his authority. He invaded Scotland, with some apparent ease, now that he was able to move freely through the north of England. The success of these various moves made it clear to others of power in Britain that their position was to be tested. They decided together to take the initiative.

A coalition led by Olaf, King of Dublin, controller of the Viking fleets and armies of Ireland, with Constantine, King of the Scots, and Owen, King of the North British, seems unlikely, and it must, when it was formed, have seemed impresssively formidable. Olaf came from Ireland with a large fleet, probably into the Mersey, a favourite haven of the Vikings. Athelstan and his brother Edmund came up through Mercia, gathering a joint Mercian and Wessex army. Constantine and Owen came south, and the whole lot met somewhere in the north-west Midlands. This speculation is based partly on the assumption that Brunaburh is the modern Bromborough, south of Bebington on the Wirrall peninsula. There and thereabouts, says the great Anglo-Saxon poem celebrating the event, the troops of the invaders were routed and systematicaly slaughtered as they fled.

> Nor was more slaughter
> On this island ever yet
> More folks killed before this
> By the sword's edge...

Olaf escaped across the sea back to Dublin, with a remnant of his force and much shame. Constantine fled to Scotland, and we are not told about Owen. Athelstan and his brother Edmund returned victorious to Wessex. And Hywel? At this critical pivot of history Hywel was not even there.

Given the fact that this was a major uprising of all the non-Saxon people, and that Hywel was effectively king of all Wales, this is surprising, to say the least. Clearly it is another symptom of his sympathy for Athelstan, or of his instinct that Wales would be better served by appeasement than by confrontation with a probably unbeatable opponent. In any case he must, we feel, have made an assessment of the situation and a conscious decision. It would be playing a diferent game to that of writing history to speculate what would have been the result if Hywel had joined the coalition; but he himself must have considered that question.

What we know is that he didn't join them, and they lost. This puts this intriguing king in the unusual position of having had a possibly profound effect on the history of Britain by something which he decided not to do.

NOTES

1. **Brut y Tywysogyon:** 'The Chronicle of the Princes', surviving in several medieval manuscripts, consists of brief records based on church annals, similar to the Annales Cambriae and the Anglo-Saxon Chronicle. It covers the period from the end of the seventh century until the death of Llywelyn ap Gruffrudd.

2. **Hywel Dda The Law,** translated and edited by Dafydd Jenkins, Gomer Press, 1990. Jenkins uses a composite text. This is the translation from which I shall be quoting further.

3. Jenkins cites this case (p. 51) and another (p. 49) as being 'survivals from a more primitively robust society'. No doubt they were taken as mere curiosities by the users of the law-books, and we cannot help wondering how they came to be left in.

Hywel is remembered for his wisdom and laws, rather than his exploits as a warrior

Owain Gwynedd

At the point at which we might have thought that internal divisions, based on ancient tribal affiliations and the old Welsh system of inheritance, had begun to be outmoded by a new pan-European impetus towards unified power, the old inbuilt tendencies re-emerge. It was, we shall see, to be not quite the last upsurge of this inherent problem, in the politics of Wales, as indeed elsewhere.

Rhodri Mawr's his son Anarawd became king of Gwynedd and founder of the House of Aberffraw. Anarawd had a son called Idwal, who rose in revolt against the Saxons and was killed; he in turn left two sons, who were forced into exile, their cousin Hywel absorbed Gwynedd into his expanding territory.

One of these sons, Iago, was later brought back, in an insecure situation on the death of Hywl Dda. Iago was assassinated by his own men, and his son Cynan seemed likely to inherit Gwynedd. This orderly process never took place, since Gwynedd then came under the power of Gruffudd ap Llywelyn, king of Deheubarth, and Cynan fled to exile in Ireland.

Cynan, perhaps best known for his absence, is often passed over in the history of this confused period. This assessment beset him from the start, since when his son Gruffudd claimed his inheritance of Gwynedd he is referred to simply as 'grandson of Iago'. There is though, I think, one important respect in which Cynan played a major role in Welsh development.

When he went to Dublin he did so as a refugee to the Danish Viking kingdom

Chepstow – the first Norman stone castle built in Wales

which ruled there. Evidently he was accepted by them as an ally, to the extent that he married into the Danish royal house. His son Gruffudd, born there, was thus half Viking, in fact the heir to two kingdoms which had up to then been enemies. It can hardly be mere chance that when he in turn ruled Gwynedd, from the late eleventh century, Viking raids on Anglesey dramatically decreased, and after some years a period of stability developed in Gwynedd which had not been possible for many years. It now began to make sense to build in stone, and several Anglesey churches have elements dating from this period of the cessation of the Viking problem.

Since Gruffudd ap Cynan's reign in Gwynedd started in 1081, he it was who first had to deal with the new enemy. Once the Normans had invaded England they spread quite quickly into southern Wales, and before long were on the northern border too, affecting Gwynedd. This development was, of course, largely a product of the feudal system, by which a king maintained his central power by delegating to the more forceful of his barons the tasks of securing the borders, particularly in their weaker areas. We thus get, quite fast, the rise of what became the Marcher Lords.

Though this became an important factor in Welsh history from then on, it was not the first problem which faced Gruffudd on his accession in Gwynedd. His first enemy was Caradog ap Gruffudd, whose ambitions extended beyond his base in Gwent, and who was a threat too to Rhys ap Tewdwr, king of Deheubarth. Gruffudd joined in alliance with Rhys, and after a significant victory the kingdoms of both Gwynedd and Deheubarth became temporarily stable.

Of signficance in the meantime is an event which took place in 1081, when Rhys met William I (described by the Welsh annals as 'king of England and Wales and much of France') at St David's cathedral, where the former was taking refuge, and the latter was on pilgrimage. It is clear that the pilgrimage had more than religious motives, since William at the same time imposed his power on the whole of southern Wales, and no doubt the meeting was not entirely accidental. The two kings agreed to recognise each others' power, albeit from rather different bases, the result of which was that Rhys was able to rule in Deheubarth at least while William lived. When he was succeeded by his son, William Rufus, things were different: William II encouraged a rival contender, and although Rhys won, the Normans had begun to be largely self-governing in south Wales, and in 1093 he was 'slain by the French who were then living in Brycheiniog' (say the Welsh annals) 'and with him fell the kingdom of the Britons'. Rhys is of interest to us in Welsh history as being the grandfather of 'The Lord Rhys' (prominent later in this chapter) and the founding ancestor of the Tudor dynasty.

Gruffudd ap Cynan, meanwhile, had succeeded after several attempts in gaining control of Gwynedd. In that situation he found himself having to deal with the earls of both Chester and Shrewsbury, both of whom were at the time called Hugh. Betrayed at a meeting with the two earls, at Rhug, near Corwen, Gruffudd then spent years imprisoned in Chester, which enabled the Earl of Chester to invade Gwynedd and build castles (for instance at Aberlleiniog) some of which still stand. Rescued from captivity and again returned to Gwynedd, Gruffudd attacked Hugh of Chester's castles with some success, and in due course, after the death of this Hugh in 1101, was in a position to come to terms with the new king of England, Henry I, who recognised his right to Gwynedd and extended his territory westwards. With increasing confidence he then pushed Gwynedd's boundaries eastwards as well, but since he was by then in his sixties it is thought that most of the later fighting was carried out by his sons – and it is at this point that Owain Gwynedd enters history.

To begin with Owain fought his father's battles together with his two brothers, Cadwallon and Cadwaladr. The former died in a battle against Powys in the 1130s, and Owain became sole ruler of Gwynedd when Cadwaladr became involved in a dispute with a rival ruler and was forced into exile. This was not until 1155, however, and we have to remember that Owain's father was still nominal ruler into his dotage (dying in 1137, aged over eighty) and by the time Owain became king of Gwynedd in his own right he was in his mid-fifties. The great success he then achieved in establishing the independence of northern Wales from the Norman barons on its border was largely due to the collapse of central power in England, the period known as the Anarchy. The implication of Owain's successes in the 1140s and 50s is that the feudal system ultimately depended on the power of the king and the national army, as a fall-back support to the Marcher Lords on England's borders.

In 1135, when Henry I died, his nephew Stephen of Blois (who had been brought up in Henry's court and already possessed much territory in England), assumed the throne, in spite of the well-known fact that Henry had designated his only surviving child, Matilda, as his heir. Matilda was married to Geoffrey of Anjou, following the death of her first husband, the Emperor Henry V: so that it was possible to portray her as a foreign power and Stephen as a native British king. This was, and proved, weak justification, and Stephen failed to gain the confidence of the powerful barons, some of whom sided with Matilda when she came in 1139 to occupy her kingdom. There were two monarchs contending for power in England then throughout the 1140s, during which period the powerful barons made treaties with each other, to the extent that central power seemed to be irrelevent (hence the term 'the Anarchy'). The Pope intervened in 1152, recognising Matilda's son Henry (the future Henry II, first of the Plantagenet kings of England) as the rightful heir, in direct line through his mother from William the Conqueror. When Stephen died in 1154 Henry Plantagenet succeeded, and the Anarchy was over.

Meanwhile Owain Gwynedd had won significant battles on his border, at Mold in 1146 and at Rhuddlan in 1150. This was to put it mildly disconcerting to the Earl of Chester at the time, Earl Ranulf, who joined forces with Owain's other threatened neighbour, Madog, Prince of

The Norman motte at Rhuddlan where Owain was victorious in 1150

Powys. Owain confronted their joint army at Coleshill, and won. For a time then he was constrained only by the feudal fall-back resource, the king's army, and while Henry was still untroubled by other distractions this was formidable. He invaded Wales with the support of Powys in 1157, meeting the Gwynedd army at Basingwerk, near Holywell, where a battle took place which nearly destroyed both leaders. Owain's army on the face of it came off best, but he was severely weakened by being at the same time threatened at remote points of his kingdom. The troops of Henry and Madog of Powys were at the same time pillaging Anglesey. Owain was obliged to come to terms. The peace (though we have no details of it) revealed the weak position of both sides. The king of England had narrowly escaped death in a wood near Basingwerk, and Owain had found himself overstretched, when Henry mustered his army in Chester and moved south along the coast to Rhuddlan. The result of the treaty was that Owain was allowed to continue to reign in Gwynedd, and Henry Plantagenet went home to London.

It emerges clearly that Owain Gwynedd was a formidable enemy to Henry II, and could not be ignored for long. He was a forceful and capable leader, and the figurehead of Welsh resistance to English encroachment during the 1160's. When Ranulf, earl of Chester, died in 1153, an opportunity occurred which Owain took to spread his power northwards. His annexation then of Tegeingl, the flat and fertile land between the rivers Dee and Clwyd, inhabited by English people in the 1160s, probably seemed to Henry a threat to the crucial border city of Chester, and he returned to the Welsh problem in 1165. He seems to have realised that the matter was best dealt with radically, since after an intitial rush to Rhuddlan, where nothing happened, he went back to England and assembled (the Welsh chronicles say) 'a host beyond number of the picked warriors of England and Normandy and Flanders and Gascony and Anjou and all the North and Scotland'. With this company, we are told, he intended to 'annihilate all Welshmen'. It was a rash ambition.

Under the supreme command of Owain Gwynedd, camped near Corwen, the men of Wales awaited the arrival of the cream of the Plantagenet empire, moving north from Oswestry. Gwynedd and Powys were now allied, following the

death of Madog in 1160, and they were supported by further forces from south Wales. The two massed armies faced each other for a time, neither willing to make the first move. It was Henry who lost patience first. He moved his forces into the Ceiriog valley, a decision which is hard to understand, but was clearly determined. He sent two thousand woodmen ahead to clear a road through the densely wooded area, but it is still not clear where they thought they were going. Presumably the intention was to outflank and perhaps encircle the outnumbered Welsh. To lead his army into a narrow valley, with the mass of the Berwyn range blocking them in on one side, was however an obvious tactical mistake. Near where Offa's dyke crosses the river Ceiriog just below Chirk castle Owain's men ambushed the English army, and Henry was lucky to escape.

He had no option but to move upwards onto the slopes of the Berwyn, where, the chronicle tells us, he stayed a few days. A few days proved too long. Something perhaps not foreseen by either side came to Owain's assistance: Wales's upland rain. Henry's gallant army fell prey not to superior forces but (in the words of the chronicle) to 'a mighty tempest of wind and bad weather and rains', and also were falling short of food. '...and then he moved his tents into England'. That was his last trip to north Wales.

It would be surpising if the major military activity under Owain's leadership had left no record on the ground, and in fact we find at this stage that constructions in earth and stone have remained for us to see. The ring forts of the pre-Saxon Iron Age had remained the basic pattern of defence, and the introduction by the Norman lords of the motte-and-bailey form was basically a refinement of this theme. Hence when we come to Tomen y Rhodwydd, near Llandegla in Denbighshire, south of Llanarmon-yn-Iâl, there is something anciently familiar about it. We know, however, that it was built by Owain in 1149, because the chronicle of the Princes tells us so: 'Owain ap Gruffudd ap Cynan built a castle in Iâl'. Strategically placed near the border of Gwynedd and Powys, and at the interface of both kingdoms with the earldom of Chester, it commands, on its plateau, the route up the Nant y Garmon valley rising from the Vale of Clwyd.

Although made of earth rather than stone, Tomen y Rhodwydd is still visibly now a magnificent structure, and when it was crowned by a large timber keep it must have presented a formidable statement. Ambitious kings from continental dynasties and upstart warlord barons should look no further. You are now in Wales.

Essentially a part of Owain's campaigns to occupy northern Powys, and at the same time to reach into Tegeingl, from this secure base he could expand and consolidate his kingdom. More than anything Tomen y Rhodwydd stands as a token of his ambitions, proclaiming still a sense of power.

Though it has become now, as earthworks do, harmonious with the surrounding countryside, one can still see the determined military layout of the castle's structure. The firmly rounded, high-piled mound and surrounding steep-sided moat proclaim its heritage from the high embankments and deep ditches of ancient British ringforts, and the way the moat winds around the bailey in a long loop shows a borrowing from Owain's Norman enemies.

In this period of relative stability provided by the cessation of the Viking onslaughts, Owain's kingdom had also begun to build in stone. This shows a confidence in the future which had so far not been apparent, in a world dominated until now by thatch and wattle. Hence some bits of churches still remain as testimony to Owain's security. At Penmon in Anglesey the Priory Church largely dates from his reign, and the fine 'Norman' arch in the church at Aberffraw is of that date too. Above the Conwy valley the simple but robust old church of Llanrhychwyn has parts belonging to the second half of the twelfth century, and several of the churches on the Llŷn peninsula have origins of that time, the elegant church of St. Beuno at Pistyll for instance having remained largely intact in twelfth-century form. Moreover by this time the Welsh themselves had begun to build castles, and it is quite possible that some early castles attributed to the Normans were in fact first built by the Welsh. Ewloe castle, for instance, largely hidden in a wood, was mainly built by his grandson Llywelyn but may have originated on a foundation initiated by Owain.[1]

When Gerald of Wales came through Gwynedd in 1188 he was shown, he says, the tomb of Owain and his brother Cadwalader in front of the high altar of Bangor cathedral, where he had been buried in recognition of his sponsorship of the cathedral. This honour, however, was in conflict with the fact that Owain had been excommunicated by the Archbishop of Canterbury, at the time Thomas Becket. The reason Becket gave was that the prince had married his own first cousin, which was forbidden in church law, and although instructed to put the marriage aside by both the Archbishop and the Pope had refused to do so. It seems likely, however, that the quarrel with Becket was already an ongoing problem. As Henry II himself was shortly to discover the Archbishop was wilful and determined, as was also indeed the king of Gwynedd. They quarrelled over the appointment of a new bishop of Bangor, Owain having appointed one himself whom Becket refused to acknowledge. Becket's nominee was prevented from taking up his office, and Bangor remained officially without a bishop for some time. In Gerald's time the bishop was under instructions to remove the prince's body from the cathedral when 'a proper opportunity' presented itself. Eight hundred and fifty years later this proper opportunity has somehow not yet presented itself, and today you can find a slate plaque set into the floor of the southern aisle which bears a rather tentative inscription: 'The body which lies interred within this wall in a stone coffin is supposed to be the remains of Owain Gwynedd', it says, 'sovereign prince of Wales', followed by some details of his career.

It seems likely that the decision by the local clergy to defy the authority of Canterbury and of Rome to give their leader an honoured burial was due to the apparent affection which his people felt for him. The *Brut y Tywysogyon* could hardly be more explicit, in its entry (in both the 'Hergest' and 'Peniarth' versions) for 1170:

> At the close of that year, in the month of November, died Owain Gwynedd ap Gruffudd ap Cynan, prince of Gwynedd, a man of great renown and of infinite prudence and nobility, the bulwark of Wales, unconquered from his youth, after victories beyond number, without having ever refused a man the request that was made to him. After taking penance and holy confession and repentance and communion of the virtues of the Body of Christ and exreme unction his soul departed to the mercy of God.

God was from the start, it seems, on Owain's side. According to Gerald the English had themselves aggravated this partisanship. When Henry II brought the vast might of the Plantagenet army to the Ceiriog valley to put an end to Wales for all time, he found himself (as we have seen) being ignominiously chased out of Wales by the weather. The day before (Gerald tells us) the English troops had been burning Welsh churches. The Welsh army was rowdy in its resentment. We hear then a rare piece of direct speech from its leader, when Owain ('a man of distinguished wisdom and moderation') addressed the troops:

> My opinion, indeed, by no means agrees with yours, for we ought to rejoice at this conduct of our adversary; for, unless supported by divine assistance, we are far inferior to the English; and they, by their behaviour, have made God their enemy, who is able most powerfully to avenge both himself and us.

1. Ceiriog river near Crogen, where Owain's army ambushed the English army; 2. A memorial plaque to the Welsh victory on the bridge at Crogen; 3. Tomen y Rhodwydd

'After which, the English army, on the following night, experienced (as has before been related) the divine vengeance.'

Gerald was in Wales, in the immediate aftermath of these events, in 1188, in the retinue of Archbishop Baldwin, archbishop of Canterbury from 1184 until his death in 1190. The expedition was part of a recruiting and fund-raising tour to promote the Third Crusade, which lasted from 1189 to 1192, and was (in theory at any rate) a response to Saladin's occupation of Jerusalem. We will be dealing with their journey in Wales in some detail shortly.

A new figure of significance rose in Wales between these times, to overshadow Owain's dominance in his last years. Rhys ap Gruffudd was the grandson of Rhys ap Tewdwr, mentioned above, and thus descended from Hywel Dda and destined to be a patriarch of the House of Tudor. He is known to us now as The Lord Rhys, which title perhaps partly recognises the anglicisation of his power. Like his forebear Hywel he made much diplomatic use of the opportunities to ally with the

The Lord Rhys' effigy at St David's cathedral

apparent enemy, the Norman English. Both Owain Gwynedd and Henry II had dealings with him, which in both cases appear to have been possibly wary and ambivalent.

Rhys had become in this pivotal position through the inheritance of a large part of south Wales. To some extent this was to begin with a nominal position, since southern Wales was in effect ruled by the Normans at the time. By the start of the 1170s, however, that is, after Owain had died, he had come to an arrangement with Henry by which he ruled south Wales with an officially recognised English title, 'Justice over South Wales' (as the entry in *Brenhidedd y Saesson: 'vstvs ar Deheubarth Kymre'*, is translated) (2). This official recognition came as the culmination of a long period of jockeying for power. In 1164 to 1167 he had allied with Owain Gwynedd against Henry, and so was part of the Welsh force which (along with the weather) sent the king unsuccessful back to England. In 1171 Rhys and Henry met at Pembroke, and again at Laugharne in 1172 (where the title mentioned above was conferred); Rhys led a force supporting the king at Tutbury in 1174, and they met a further eight times between 1174 and 1185.

It is easy to see why Henry would wish to placate Rhys, but harder to see why he felt able to trust him. In the attempt to restore the Norman lords to their territories in Ceredigion and Llandovery Henry intervened with royal support four times between 1158 and 1163, and each time Rhys capitulated – and each time he renewed his attempts to expel the Normans as soon as the king was gone. It must in the end have seemed more practical to have Rhys working for him rather than against him. Thus officially recognised as ruler of Deheubarth, Rhys held the balance in Wales between the Marcher lords and the residual independent kngdoms, favoured in this by the chaotic cirumstances of Gwynedd after Owain died.

Interestingly Gerald speaks highly of him, and since Rhys accompanied him and the archbishop right through Ceredigion he had the opportunity to know him personally, and was (as he is keen to point out) in any case related to him, Gerald's grandmother being Rhys's aunt, making them (I think) first cousins once removed. Gerald praises his cousin for his 'natural kindness and civility' and for exhbiting 'a liberality peculiarly praiseworthy in so illustrious a prince'.

During the last years of this time King Henry had his own separate problems (which may help to explain why he chose to placate Rhys at this point rather than attempt to weaken him). Henry had arranged for Thomas Becket, formerly his chancellor and loyal friend, to be ordained a priest, in 1162, and immediately had him consecrated Archbishop of Canterbury, in succession to Theobald, who had died. This was evidently part of a plan to gain greater control of the church, but much to the king's displeasure it didn't work. For the next two years the new archbishop resolutely opposed him. The matters of dissent seem often pedantic, but it was the spirit of rebellion which rankled. Henry accused Becket of misconduct while chancellor, and the cleric, taking this as a warning, fled in disguise to France. The Pope and the French king urged Henry and Thomas to become reconciled, but neither would trust the other. Becket came back to England in 1170, and while Henry was in Normandy some knights in his retinue crossed to England and murdered the archbishop in his cathedral, in December 1170. Hardly surpisingly this proved no solution, and dangerously increased the king's unpopularity.

The effect of all this is that for much of the 1160s and some of the 1170s Henry was embroiled in controversy which diverted his attention from territorial politics. Ironically (as we have seen) Owain Gwynedd had earlier had his own battle of wills with the same Archbishop. That the two kings should be confronted by much the same problem is an illustration of the extent to which the central power of the church had become supranational.

It is one of the great pieces of historical good fortune that Gerald wrote the whole thing down. We get a wide and rich insight into the way of life in twelfth century Wales made all the more sharp for us by the fact that he himself found it all – John Davies calls him 'the first non-Welsh-speaking Welshman' – almost as strange as we do now.

When Gerald and the archbishop enter Wales from Hereford we feel they are conscious of being in a foreign country. The Welsh did not at that time speak English, so there was a constant need for an interpreter. We have to remember that Gerald, whose mother was half-Welsh, had been brought up in Norman parts of south Wales, educated at Gloucester and in Paris, and had appointments from the see of Canterbury and the royal court, where he became a clerk to the king. Although he is known to us, and to history, as Giraldus Cambrensis, Gerald of Wales, due to his having been born in Manorbier in what is now Pembrokeshire, he was by heritage mainly Norman, son of William de Barri who had obtained land in the Vale of Glamorgan before moving to Pembrokeshire, and grandson on his mother's side of Gerald de Windsor, the Norman Constable of Pembroke castle. De Windsor had married Nest, the daughter of Rhys ap Tewdwr, descendant of Hywel Dda, who provides the only completely Welsh bit of Gerald's ancestry.

It is clear that Gerald and Baldwin and their retinue did not feel any hostility as foreigners, in spite of the background of historic antagonism and ongoing politcal distrust. Conflict appears to have been more internal than international, however: 'The natives of these parts, actuated by continual enmities and implacable hatred, are perpetually engaged in bloody contests.'

They were met at once by The Lord Rhys, 'prince of South Wales', who became so persuaded by the archbishop's sermon that he decided to undertake the crusade himself, but in spite of preparing for two weeks 'for so distant a journey' was talked out of it by his wife. The Itinerary in general reveals to us a deeply superstitious world, in which holy relics have miraculous properties and strange things happen, which Gerald reports with evident total credulity. His account of the journey is enlivened by local gossip, loaded with stories of great wonders and improbable events.

Politically Gerald's background inclines him (though revisiting as part of the English delegation) to emphasise instances of English recogntion of Welsh rights, as when Henry I was moved by a story to observe that although 'we commit acts of violence and wrong against these people, yet they are known to be the rightful inheritors of this land'. Politically, at that time, southern and central Wales are seen as unsettled countries, beset by local feuds and conflicts. Much of this unrest (but not, as we have seen, all) is between the Normans and the Welsh, (the 'governors of castles ... against the natives').

Crowds flocked to hear the archbishop's sermons and receive the cross, the whole thing being 'explained to the Welsh by an interpreter'. It is clear, looking around, that the country was not just self-sustaining but even engaged in export business – the forest of Dean, which they passed when moving between Caerleon and Newport, 'amply supplied Gloucester with iron and venison'. Much of Roman Caerleon was at that time intact, and Gerald wonders at it: a 'city of undoubted antiquity, and handsomely built of masonry, with courses of bricks, by the Romans.'

> Many vestiges of its former splendour may yet be seen; immense palaces formerly ornamented with gilded roofs, ... a tower of prodigious size, remarkable hot baths, relics of temples and theatres, all inclosed within fine walls, parts of which remain standing. ... and what I think worthy of notice, stoves contrived with wonderful art, to transmit the heat insensibly through narrow tubes up the side walls.

We learn much detail of twelfth-century Wales on the journey, and many facts beyond that – for instance that Henry II had a freckled face. The constant need to translate the business of the expedition into Welsh is not just an instance of the foreigness, to them, of Wales. There was, it is clear, a general diversity of language in Brtain at that time. Gerald tells us that when Henry II, returning from Ireland, visited Cardiff, he was confronted by a monk who addressed him in the English of the time ('the teutonic tongue'), and Henry had to ask in French the man who was holding his horse to translate his part of the conversation 'in English'. Gerald often refers to the Normans in Wales as 'the English' ('the English standing on one side, and the Welsh on the other'), but explicitly contrasts the languages of 'English' and 'French', only one of which, it is clear, was spoken by the Norman nobility. The archbishop's sermons and exhortations were, he says, delivered to the assembled people 'both in the Latin and French tongues', with on one occasion at least a local archdeacon 'acting as interpreter to the Welsh', but even with no interpreter the oratory seemd sufficient to impress 'those person who understood neither of those languages', because both linguistic groups signed up, for the enterprise, the crusade.

At Haverfordwest Gerald records the Flemish origin of the population: they were planted there by Henry I, and although 'ever hostile to the Welsh' thrived through the woollen industry.

On they went, via St. David's to Cardigan, where they were 'handsomely entertained by prince Rhys', then on through rural mid-Wales, noting the salmon leaps on the Teifi, the only river in Wales which had beavers, and they entered north Wales across the river Dyfi, where The Lord Rhys, who had accompanied them through Cardiganshire, left them and went home. Owain Gwynedd's grandson Gruffudd then attended them.

Across Traeth Mawr and Traeth Bychan to Caernarfon and by a mountain track to Bangor. An excursion to Anglesey, then back to Bangor and on to Conwy, crossing the river by boat 'leaving the Cistercian monastery of Conwy on the western bank of the river on our right hand'. Sometimes the roads are no more than tracks, often precarious, with the need for local guidance. In due course they cross the Dee and enter Chester, and by way of Oswestry and Shrewsbury return to Hereford, where the remarkable journey ends, come full circle.

Fascinating as the passing details are, it is really Gerald's follow-up, the

Description of Wales, which sets out for us as clearly as he can describe it what Wales was like, and what it was like to live there, in the time of Owain Gwynedd and The Lord Rhys. His aim is 'to give some account of this my native country, and to describe the genius of its inhabitants, so entirely distinct from that of other nations'. It is, as he describes it, a pleasant and fertile country, eight days' journey long and four days' journey wide.

His report on the population reads like that of an anthropologist studying a distant culture, and he shows what seems to us a modern scientific habit of making a careful analysis of the prevailing facts. He observes that Wales is mainly agricultural and self-sufficient – 'almost all the people live upon the produce of their herds... They pay no attention to commerce, shipping, or manufactures...' – their husbandry being only interrupted by warfare (of which there seems to have been plenty). He quotes the king himself, Henry II, as having identified the Welsh as bold and fierce, desperate and untameable. Gerald himself sees them as characteristcally preoccupied with the security of their country and possessions, diligent and temperate ('not addicted to gluttony or drunkennness') and much given to hospitality. It seems on the surface to be a good place in which to be a passing stranger. You leave your weapons at the door, and you then get your feet washed, and young women are assigned to make conversation and to play the harp to you. The austerity which lies behind this however soon begins to temper its pleasantness.

Your hosts would be conscientiously attentive, when it came to the evening meal, not touching a thing themselves until all the guests were satisfied, but this was for fear of provision falling short; the dishes served were few and rather plain, supplemented by freshly-baked bread. Sometimes the meal also included a sort of stew.

These meals are taken in rather sparse surroundings, since there are no tables, cloths, or napkins. Guests are seated in groups of three, with all the dishes presented at the same time, and placed, in large platters, on rushes and grass. When bedtime comes it takes the form of beds made of rushes set along the sides of the

On Gerald's journey: 1. Dyfi estuary; 2. Brecon cathedral; 3. St David's cathedral room, on which a blanket made of coarse cloth is the only bedding, so that, sleeping in their day clothes, the guests took comfort from the natural heat generated by nearby sleepers and from the fact that the central fire burned all night, so that when the cold became serious they could get up and stand by it, then when recovered go back to their hard and chilly beds.

The enormous detail whch Gerald gives us implies that it is not at all what visitors might be used to, or he himself, come from his normal life at court or at the castles of the Norman lords.

His account of the physical surroundings of austerity continues with an equally detailed analysis of the personal appearance and habits of the peole who lived in these conditions. Men and women both wore their hair quite short, clear of the ears and the eyes. They are unusually fussy about their teeth, polishing them until they are like ivory with green hazel and a woollen cloth. The men shave off their beards, but retain moustaches. They are sharp-witted and quick to learn, skilled musicians and skilled in poetry and rhetoric.

One peculiarity he finds worth dwelling on is the presence of people 'whom you will find nowhere else' who are in a state of inspiration. They behave as if possessed by a spirit, subject to violent fits which sound like epileptic seizures. People believe them to have mystical knowledge, though they receive wildly incoherent answers to their questions, which they then have to interpret ingeniously, as one did with the Delphic oracle. We inevitably recognise the figure of the mad prophet of folklore and early literature, and indeed Gerald mentions Merlin at this point.

The Welsh, he says are much concerned with their pedigrees: 'even the common people retain their genealogy' to the sixth or seventh generation or beyond, a feature of social life which might stem from the legal systems set out (for instance) in the Law of Hywel Dda. They are not, he says, an urban people, but live in wattle huts in the woods. Their farmland is mainly pasture. The bit which is arable is ploughed by four yolked oxen. For fishing they use a hide-covered stick-framed vessel which they carry on their backs to the rivers, clearly a coracle.

Gerald, in the first part of his 'Description', has shown us a commendable and moderate people, but he sees, he says, that he must also tell the truth of the Welsh people's flaws. 'No man is born without faults...' and it should not be offensive to mention them. The Welsh are not too scrupulous about telling the truth, when a lie would better suit their purpose. Moreover the Welsh, he says, conceive it right to commit acts of theft and robbery. They are not even, nowadays, brave fighters: after a big and noisy show of defiance in the first attack, they then 'trust to flight for safety'. They are not beaten so easily, however, because they then, instead of open warfare, rely on guerrilla tactics.

They do not respect agreed conditions of land tenure, but seek to enlarge their occupied holdings by ignoring boundaries, a feature which may have been of concern, on a larger scale, to the Marcher Lords.

Gerald points to a possible cause of these flaws, perhaps derived from the sense of the importance of genealogy: inbreeding. Incest, he says , is not something of which they are ashamed. He is in fact quite clear about the motives: from 'their love of high descent' they 'unite themselves to their own people, refusing to intermarry with strangers.'

Having asssured himself that it is not offensive to mention a population's faults, Gerald then gets a little carried away. He hints that it was divine vengeance for 'that detestable and wicked vice of Sodom' which deprived the Welsh of the rest of Britain. We begin to feel the possibility of the insertion of Norman propaganda when he sums the appraisal up: the Welsh 'cannot be said to have repented, when we see them involved in such an abyss of vices, perjury, theft, robbery, rapine, murders, fratricides, adultery, and incest...'

Reinforcing this feeling of political editing, we find Gerald saying that the few things the Welsh are proud of 'are more properly to be attributed to the diligence and activity of the Norman kings than to their own merits or power.' Before the Normans came the English tried to wipe them out. Now, he says, they have recovered their lands and thrown off the yoke which had been imposed on them. If the Normans wish to subdue them he advises playing on their principal weakness by stirring up internal enmity, 'knowing the spirit of hatred and envy which generally prevails amongst them...' Thus by local knowledge coupled with sanctions on trade the people may be subdued. Once brought under Norman power the region should be governed with moderation, Gerald tells history. It was to be, of course, a further hundred years before such a state of affairs took place.

He (or whoever wrote the uncharacteristic political passages towards the end of his book) sees the Welsh as being in a barbarous state and having no principle of honour. They have to be coerced into reasonable behaviour, and he warns against geater trust. The final chapters are of interest to us as a revelation of the complacent and patronising attitude of the Norman invaders. However perhaps we should recognise too some traces of objective appraisal. Three factors, Gerald states, held Wales back at that time: the division of inheritance between all the sons of the deceased; an educational system which fostered patronage; and a resistance to the principle of centralised government: 'because from the pride and obstinacy of their disposition, they will not (like other nations) subject themselves to the dominion of one lord and king.'

Historical generalisations are seldom true, and we find in fact that last remark to be a bit contradicted by the subject matter of this chapter. The Welsh do appear to have been willing to accept the central power personified by Owain Gwynedd. John Davies makes an interesting point (pp. 128-9) when he says that Owain's title of king (*rex*) of Gwynedd was inferior to the other title he was known by, prince (*princeps*) of the Welsh. Owain had (for instance) led the forces of all Wales against Henry II. 'These titles are important, for they provide virtually the only evidence of the way in which the Welsh rulers viewed themselves and of the way in which their status was interpreted by the outside world.' We shall have reason to refer to this question of terms again in relation to the two Llywelyns.

Wales's threats and adversaries had changed step by step during the course of Owain's ancestry – from emergent Angle and Saxon kingdoms, through Viking incursions and the resulting Danish power-blocks, then with the radical upheaval of the arrival of the Normans and their conquest of the territories relatively recently established in the rest of Britain, all in the space of some three hundred years. Yet through all this Wales had retained its own identity and its determined pursuit of its independence. Now it was clear that the matter of who lived, and ruled, in the whole of the island south of Scotland was a question of the confrontation of the Welsh and a heterogeneous patchwork of people misleadingly termed by those recording this process as 'the English'.

NOTES

1. **Built heritage.** *Much of the subject matter of these paragraphs is dealt with also in my book* North Wales in the Making, *published by Gwasg Carreg Gwalch, 2003; pp. 128, 129.*

2. **Brenhinedd y Saesson.** *'The Kings of the Saxons' is one version of the Chronicles of the Princes, the Brut y Tywysogyon mentioned in an earlier note. The 'Hergest' version has him appointing* yr Arglwydd Rhys yn iustus yn holl Deheubarth; *the 'Peniarth' manuscript mentions the meeting at Laugharne, but not the appointment.*

Llywelyn Fawr

When Owain Gwynedd died in 1170 it immediately became clear that he had omitted to secure a smooth succession. He had a number of sons, and may have assumed that the ruling of Gwynedd would be taken on by the eldest of them, although, absurd as this may seem, it was not unquestionably clear who this was. This situation arose because a number of his sons were illegitimate, in some cases because they were the offspring of one or other of his several mistresses, but more significantly because one of his two marriages was declared invalid by the Catholic church, since Cristin, his second wife, was his first cousin. His son Rhun was the eldest by Cristin, and the one most likely to have been chosen as heir by Owain, but Rhun died long before his father, in 1146. Then the choice fell on Hywel, and indeed he was the one who appears to have expected to rule. Hywel however was challenged by his brothers Dafydd and Rhodri, fled to Ireland and when he came back with an Irish army was killed by them at the battle of Pentraeth, in Anglesey.

That left Maelgwn and Iorwerth, the eldest sons of his first wife Gwladus, who seem to have been assumed to be supplanted by the subsequent marriage. Maelgwn died while the matter was still disputed, in 1173. That left Iorwerth.

Iorwerth was indisputably legitimate and entitled to inherit, being the eldest son of the first marriage, and quite why this did not take place has always required an explanation. We find Iorwerth active in south Wales at this time, while the rival groups of brohers and half-brothers were sharing out Gwynedd. Gerald of Wales, writing about the state of the country which resulted, mentions Iorwerth's nickname: Drwyndwn, 'which in Welsh means flat-nosed', implying that perhaps some childhood accident had left him deformed. '… for which defect,' as W. Llewelyn Williams puts it in his 1908 edition of Gerald's 'Itinerary', 'he was deemed unfit to preside over the principality of North Wales and was deprived of his rightful inheritance, which was seized by his brother David…' This is the traditionally accepted explanation, supported, for instance, by John Davies in the modern literature, in *A History of Wales*: 'kings had to be without blemish'.

Whatever the cause, this led to the following situation in northern Wales: Cynan was lord of Meirionnydd, which was shared afer his death (in 1174) by his two sons, Gruffudd and Maredudd; Rhodri, Dafydd's full brother, ruled Anglesey and Arfon, until expelled from these by his nephews, the above sons of Cynan; Maelgwn, half-brother from the first marriage, had a claim on Anglesey, but was exiled from there to Ireland and on his return imprisoned; Iorwerth had received Arfon and apparently Nant Conwy, but does not appear in person and probably died about 1174 in exile, perhaps in England. The great kingdom of Owain Gwynedd seemed quite suddenly to have fallen apart. But Iorwerth, Gerald tells us, 'had a son named Llywelyn' and he, Gerald makes clear, was the rightful legitimate heir. With evident hindsight he adds that Llywelyn's eventual success is 'proof that adulterous and incestuous persons are displeasing to God'.

> This young man, being only twelve years of age, began, during the period of our journey to molest his uncles Dafydd and Rhodri, the sons of Owain by Christiana, his cousin-german.

It is thought that Gerald is exaggerating slightly about Llywelyn's precocity, since dating would appear to show that he was fourteen or fifteen at the time of his arrival in Gwynedd, rather than twelve (although elsewhere it was said that he was in arms by the age of ten). Fourteen, though it is extraordinary to us now, was a recognised age in the Middle Ages for a man of high birth to become active in conflict and politics. Richard II, for instance, was fourteen when he personally confronted the rebel leaders during the Peasants' Revolt. His father, the Black Prince, was sixteen when he won the crucial battle of Crecy. Henry IV had entrusted his son Hal, the future Henry V, with command of the royal forces in Wales in the war against Owain Glyndŵr at the age of sixteen.

To some extent Dafydd, by his ruthless purging of his brothers and cousins, had made it easier for Llywelyn to clear up the confusion. Dafydd had, by the time Llywelyn became active in his task of unifying Gwynedd, done quite a lot of the work for him. Moreover Llywelyn had on his side a good number of disaffected cousins. Gerald, who seems conscious that Llywelyn himself would read his report, says that 'within a few years' (from 1188) Llywelyn 'bravely expelled from North Wales those who were born in public incest' – but from the chronicles it is clear that it took much longer than that. It was 1194 (by which time he was in his early twenties) before he, with his cousins the sons of Cynan, and his uncle Rhodri, triumphed over Dafydd at a battle apparently on the Conwy estuary, 'and', says the chronicle, 'they expelled him from all his territory except for three castles.' These, David Moore reasons, in his useful work *The Welsh Wars of Independence*, would be in Tegeingl or Dyffryn Clwyd.[1] Shortly after this, in 1197, Dafydd was exiled further, and eventually withdrew to his lands in the Welsh Marches, near Ellesemere, where he and his son Owain remained for the rest of their lives.

Llywelyn was then left with only his cousin Gruffudd, son of Cynan, as rival. He defeated Gruffudd, with whom he had sided in the expulsion of Dafydd, at a battle in 1199. This was the start of a long succession of campaigns against those who had been his allies, and sometimes with those who had been his enemies, which leaves us,

now, puzzled as to how sides could be changed so easily in Wales at that time. Llywelyn did not kill or expel Gruffudd, however, since the latter died at the Abbey of Aberconwy, having become a monk there, in 1200. At that point it may be said that Llywelyn was in a dominant position in Gwynedd, then aged twenty-eight.

Besides the reference by Gerald to his precocious start we know little of Llywelyn's life before his appearance on the world stage. It is reasonably assumed that after his father's death he was brought up among his mother's kin in northern Powys. The legend that he was born in Dolwyddelan castle is probably not true, and may be the residue of a wish to make him more legitimately connected with Gwynedd when he first appears there. Certainly there was an older castle near the present one, which may have dated from the time his father controlled that area. Iorwerth is noted, however, for his absence. We hear of him seldom at around the time of Llywelyn's birth, and always in connection with south Wales.

From about the middle of the twelfth century the *Brut y Tywysogyon*, the Welsh

Tŵr Llywelyn, in the town walls of Conwy, incorporated by Edward I in his defences

annals, becomes increasingly detailed. There we find, from 1200 to about 1236, Llywelyn almost continually at war, with his rivals in Wales, with Wales's neighbouring Normans, with the English king. Attempts to map the details of these campaigns, working from the annals, are plentiful, but show no overall pattern, only the pragmatism of a capable and tireless adversary. There are factors of significance for Wales which emerge from the turmoil. One is the prince's relations with King John, a matter of some intriguing complexity. Another is his dealings with the church.

While Richard I was king of England the Welsh princes mainly had contact with his representatives, the Marcher Lords. The king spent most of his reign out of the country. When he was back he had much catching up to do, and it was in the course of trying to sort out a minor insurrection that he died, shot by a bolt from the castle he was besieging. That was in April, 1199. His brother John succeeded him, and at once things were quite different in Wales.

John was himself a Marcher Lord. He

Dolwyddelan castle – Llywelyn's supposed birthplace

held lands in Gloucestershire, through his marriage to Isobel, the Gloucester heiress. Although the attempt to hold on to the sprawling Angevin empire occupied much of his reign, and ultimately failed, he had the interest and the inclination to attend to matters in Wales. This evidently brought him into personal contact with its most powerful leader, Llywelyn. The two men probably felt they had something in common, in that each had had to manipulate their way out of a quarrelsome and complex family background.

To begin with Llywelyn was more preoccupied with securing his internal borders than with confronting the power of England. He had kinship ties with the rulers of northern Powys, but further south there was a problem in the person of Gwenwynwyn, prince of southern Powys. In 1202 Llywelyn made a decisive move. He took a considerable army into southern Powys. This assault was not in the end the success he had hoped for, and a peace treaty with Gwenwynwyn was the only outcome.

Evidently John observed all this with interest. It seems that Powys was seen as more of a threat to the English border than Gwynedd, and to begin with he supported Llywelyn against his rival. In the end it becomes apparent that what he wanted was to weaken both their powers, and John's support shifted when either of them became too strong. Llywelyn appeared, during the early thirteenth century, to be winning this game, if so perhaps due to his superior gift for diplomacy. He took an oath of loyalty to King John in 1201. In 1204 he went to do him homage. So effective were these marks of friendship in fact that the same year the king offered the prince the hand of his daughter.

This surprising alliance between the royal houses of these two neighbouring countries had enduring consequences. It was not, as it happens, the first event of its kind. Llywelyn's uncle Dafydd had married in 1174 the half-sister of Henry II, Emma, a natural daughter of Geoffrey of Anjou. On that occasion the English king had given him as dowry the Ellesmere lands to which he was eventually exiled, and it is a nice point of irony that John now gave as dowry to Llywelyn those same lands, which had reverted to the Crown on the death of Dafydd.

Joan was King John's daughter by an unknown mother. Turvey reasons that because she was brought from Normandy to England in 1205 she had probably spent her formative years in France, where her father's control of the Dukedom of Normandy and the terrritories in Anjou fell apart in 1204.[2] Although the marriage was proposed by John and had undoubted political intentions, there can be no doubt (as we shall see) that it developed into a romantic personal liaison. Its double function then continued, since (evidently a powerful and spirited personality) she acted as a valuable intermediary between the two rulers, her husband and her father, and on the death of John with her half-brother too, the young Henry III.

For a time at least this exercise in diplomacy paid off well for Llywelyn. Gwenwynwyn was arrested by the king at Shrewsbury, and Llywelyn, taking his cue, annexed his territory. This sent shivers of fear through Wales, and castles were burnt rather than risk his possessing them. Llywelyn at this point seemed unstoppable. It is probably about that point that King John realised his mistake.

He had in fact by then made several. One was perhaps that of dispossessing William de Braose, head of a powerful Marcher family, ruling Brecon, Radnor, Builth and Abergevenny. He and his wife and son took refuge in Ireland. When the king came there on an Irish campaign in 1210 he took the opportunity to return to Wales. It was probably that move which set in motion the chain of events which was to lead Llywelyn into war.

Something , at any rate, set off that year hostilities between Llywelyn and the Earl of Chester. Whatever the underlying cause, the immediate issue was the castle at Deganwy. This had originally been built as early as the eleventh century by Robert of Rhuddlan, a Norman Marcher Lord. A later castle built by Llywelyn himself had since been destroyed for fear of its possible use by King John. In 1210 the Earl of Chester rebuilt it.

This was, to Llywelyn, a blatant act of provocation, and accordingly he set about ravaging the Earl's territory. But that in turn stirred the king to action, and John not only mustered a royal army to (as he thought) destroy Llywelyn's power for ever, but assembled as his allies the remaining princes of Wales. Gwenwynwyn was restored in the process, in one of those sudden reversals of favour which seem so odd to us but were apparently taken as normal practice at the time. The king's army and the princes of mid and south Wales met at Chester, and proceeded to march into the Perfeddwlad, the fertile and open eastern borders of Gwynedd.

Perhaps the most characteristic military quality which the Welsh had in the middle ages, and indeed before, was complete mobility. They did not live in established towns or build durable buildings. Their agriculture was mainly pastoral, and so could be easily moved. King John must have been initially surprised to find he could march his vast army through northern Wales unopposed. There was no-one there.

Llywelyn, the chronicle tells us, had 'removed both his people and their chattels to the mountains of Eryri'. It was a realistic thing to do, since it must have been obvious that Llywelyn with presumably a small and ill-equipped fighting force could not take on the full might of England. But the ploy contained a secret weapon too, since it undermined one of the principles of medieval military campaigns. Large armies on the move could not, without encumbrance, carry their supplies with them. They depended mainly on pillaging the grounds they overran. Anything there might have been, however, in the Perfeddwlad, had gone into the mountains with Llywelyn and his people. Just as there was no one there to block their way, there was nothing to eat either.

They must have thought that things would improve if they went on, because the whole lot marched on as far as Deganwy castle. Possibly by then they had any lines of supply cut off behind them. It was a classic strategic blunder.

> And there the host suffered such lack of food that an egg was sold for a penny-halfpenny; and it was a luxurious feast for them to have the flesh of their horses. And because of that the king returned to England about Whitsun with his mission unfulfilled, having ignominiously lost many of his men and of his chattels.

So reports the Hergest version of the *Brut*. John had, however, learnt a lesson. When he came again in August it was with plenty of supplies, and by a different route.

This time King John avoided the stalemate of the confrontation with the Conwy river at Deganwy. He approached from the Oswestry direction and so could cross the river higher up. Once over the Conwy he had his troops in the heartland of Gwynedd, and he made this point by burning the city of Bangor and capturing its bishop. Bishop Rhobert in due course ransomed himself by paying two hundred falcons.

With the king now deep inside his territory Llywelyn was prompted to urgent action. He decided to use his most powerful weapon. He 'sent to the king his wife, who was daughter to the king, to make peace between him and the king on whatsoever terms she could.' Hardly surprisingly, given this brief, the terms were not good for the Welsh.

Llywelyn lost the right to the Perfeddwlad, his territory east of the Conwy, and suffered a fine of twenty thousand cattle and forty horses. He also gave hostages from noble families, including evidently a son of his own.[3] It is no wonder that 'the king returned victorious with great joy to England'.

Almost all the Welsh princes had allied with John against Llywelyn, but when the king started building castles in Wales after the peace treaty they began to doubt the

One of the hills of Deganwy castle above the Conwy estuary

wisdom of that. John was not to be a distant ruler, clearly, but a present threat. With what looks like fickleness, but might perhaps more objectively be viewed as pragmatism, they once again united under Llywelyn. They took all the king's new castles in Gwynedd (probably wooden invasion forts) except Deganwy and Rhuddlan, the two older stone-built structures. As long as he still held these King John still had a grip on Gwynedd.

At this point another strange anomaly took place, and with it a shift of key in the play of interaction between the two wilful leaders. Llywelyn spent the Easter of 1212 with his father-in-law and recent enemy at Cambridge. This was during the brief period of peace following his fine and before the Welsh rose once again in revolt, but it nevertheless seems an unlikely outcome of the recent war. Sir John Lloyd, in his 1911 book *A History of Wales to the Edwardian Conquest*, gives the opinion that the Cambridge visit might have been a causal factor in the insurrection. Having seen the state of affairs at the English court, Sir John says, 'Llywelyn thus learnt

that he had no reason to fear a second invasion...' King John was, to put it mildly, in a weak position. He was barely clinging to his throne, largely in the power of hostile and determined barons. Subsequent events certainly suggest that at some point Llywelyn became aware of this. If it became apparent at Easter it would explain why by the end of June the Welsh leaders had revolted.

John was in the north at the time – on 28th June he was at Durham. Llywelyn had recovered the borderland by the time he got to Chester. It looked for a time as if Llywelyn had miscalculated, and an invasion was imminent. But the king still had to keep an eye over his shoulder. He received letters revealing a plot by the barons to betray him during the Welsh campaign. It is possible, of course, and this must have occurred to him, that the Welsh uprising was itself a part of that conspiracy. At any rate on 16th August he called the campaign off.

That year in fact, 1212, was the start of Llywelyn's absolute rule in Gwynedd and over much of Wales – the end of the long period of manoevre and dissent which had kept him in uncertainty for most of his life. Early in 1213 he took the castles of

Llywelyn Fawr's statue at Conwy town centre

Deganwy and Rhuddlan. By 1214 King John, threatened with civil war, was turning to the Welsh princes for their support. Far from his getting this, his isolated position encouraged Llywelyn and Gwenwynwyn to join forces with the northern rebels. By this time they had the church on their side as well: in 1212 the Pope had formally absolved them from their oaths of allegiance to King John, and he went so far as to tell them that in expiation of their sins they should war against the iniquity of the king. In 1215 Llywelyn and his Welsh army, playing now on the international stage, took Shrewsbury – or rather it fell to them without resistance. By the end of 1215 he had taken all the royal centres in south Wales, and as it was a mild winter he was able to campaign right through it. On 26th December he was moving up again through mid Wales, and took the royal strongholds of Cardigan and Cilgerran.

By then, of course, events signficant to history were happening next door. Unlike his predecessor John spent most of his time in Britian. His atempts to retain and then to regain the Angevin lands in France involved sporadic visits there, but these were little more than that. England was his home kingdom, and he ruled it with some considerable personal application. Conscious of the bad press which John has consistently, and no doubt deservedly, received, some modern historians strive to emphasise the considerable energy and conscientiousness he displayed in running his country. *The Oxford Companion to British History* summarises this trend: 'John has come to appear in a new light as a very capable administrator with great powers of organization and application.' It is recognised, this summary says, that he 'was a very intelligent and able man.' How then did it all go so badly wrong?

Part of the problem was the ambiguous view of kingship which prevailed at the time, and indeed for the next few hundred years. The concept of an absolute monarch had never really been free of qualification. A king had to do his job, protect his people, curtail his personal excesses. The problematic nature of John's reign was certainly due in part to his own temperament. He was capable of great cruelty and of fits of temper. One of the major factors which affected the power of kings was the need for money, a problem which crops up in English history again and again. The medieval monarch had some income of his own from feudal lands, but all kings had to ask their subjects to fund national expenditure, which by now was increasingly burdened by a large body of administrators, the equivalent of the Civil Service.

In theory the feudal system demanded the free supply of troops as part of its deal, but in practice this had frequently become commuted into 'scutage', shield-money, a form of tax. This had become independent of national emergencies (which was what it was for) and took the form of a sort of wealth tax, which John exploited. The monarch, John included, then hired mercenaries. Scutage alone could not be relied on to fund something as expensive as the French wars, and it became necessary to impose other forms of tax. In this John was inventive. He introduced a type of inheritance tax and a form of income tax, sold official positions (along with their opportunities for exploitation), charged for granting charters, levied import and export taxes, and imposed a special tax on Jews.

It seems the barons in the north of England reached the inevitable point of resistance first, having no vested interest in the recovery of the French territories and yet being expected to pay towards attempts at that. When the French campaign failed in 1214 and John returned to London in October, he found a mood of rebellion setting in. In January 1215 he undertook discussions with the rebel barons, but in the end his efforts to maintain peace proved inadequate. By June a rebel army had marched on London. The king and the rebel leaders met at Runnymede on 15th June. This was a water-meadow by the Thames not far from Windsor (*inter Windlesoram et Stanes*, 'between Windsor and Staines'), which was a place traditionally used from the time of Alfred the Great to hold meetings.

There King John agreed to Magna Carta. This (though its terms were largely ignored in the short term by both sides) represents something of a turning point in British history. It is chiefly the act of its taking place at all, the fact of a king being obliged to enter a formal contract with his subjects, that changed the *de facto* constitution. The clauses of the deed itself are partly concerned with severely constraining the power of the Crown. It set out concessions which redressed some of the main complaints of the barons who had brought this situation about, such as the 'scutage' tax, which was thence to be limited to specific cases, and otherwise to be assessed ('to obtain the general consent of the realm') by the calling of the prototype of a parliament. But all this concerns us here because Llywelyn's requirements too were incorporated in the Charter. It forms an official recognition of the fact that Wales, along with Scotland, was a force which the king of England had to take into account.

Clauses 56 to 58 of the Magna Carta set out what amounts to a reversal of the deprivations carried out against the Welsh by John himself and his immediate forebears, Henry II, his father, and Richard I his brother. Forfeited lands were to be returned 'according to the laws of Wales'. In fact the separation of the legal systems was to be recognised:

> English law shall apply to holdings of land in England, Welsh law to those in Wales, and the law of the Marches to those in the Marches. The Welsh shall treat us and ours in the same way.

Welsh hostages which John himself had taken (presumably after his successful campaign in Gwynedd in 1211) were to be returned immediately:

> We will at once return the son of Llywelyn, all Welsh hostages, and the charters delivered to us as security for the peace.

By this time Llywelyn was aged forty-three, and was the undisputed ruler of a nation. In 1216 he called a Parliament at Aberdyfi, at which, with remarkable sagacity, he shared out the districts of Wales among his fellow princes, keeping nothing for himself. His position was as overlord of them all. It is as if Llywelyn had taken note of John's predicament and was not going to let it happen to him. This strategy, if it was such, succeeded. Under the protection of his personal power life in Wales was allowed a period of flourishing.

Peering at it now through the hazy lens of history, to us early thirteenth-century Wales seems a pleasant enough place. We have learnt from Gerald what it looked like. It is a land in which there was almost no concept of a town. The nearest features it had seen to urbanisation were the Roman camps, the surrounding shanty-towns of which must have given them an

1. Cardigan castle; 2. Cilgerran castle; 3. Shrewsbury castle

urban nature when they were in use. Now only the ruined vestiges of them remained. In the Marches, at Chester, Shrewsbury and Hereford, Norman lordships, bringing with them the apparatus of knights and retainers, had developed into administrative centres. In Wales itself Llywelyn's courts and castles were based more on the model of the Roman villa, homesteads in a rural land.

Just as his subjects were characterised by their mobility, being able to uproot and move wholesale into the mountain fastness, so Llywelyn and his court were itinerant too. In his absence a common court administered justice and kept order in each commote, but higher cases awaited the arrival of the prince. Although he personaly was the ultimate law-giver, he was advised by a formal council consisting of specific officers.

Chief among Llywelyn's entourage was his 'distain' or seneschal, Ednyfed Fychan, a man who became a force in Wales in his own right and set up a dynasty which to a large extent established the future squirearchy. He became head of Llywelyn's

Llys Euryn, the site of Ednyfed Fychan's residence

court in about 1218, the year in which he was present at the signing of the Treaty of Worcester. He is referred ot as 'steward' when witnessing charters in 1225 and 1230. Ednyfed himself held lands in northern Gwynedd, at Llandrillo, near the present Rhos on Sea, where his residence was destroyed by Owain Glyndŵr and subsequently replaced by a substantial stone-built house the ruins of which may still be seen at the base of Bryn Euryn. His lands extended to the seashore at Rhos Fynach, where the original church of Dinerth was lost to inundation and the parish moved to Llandrillo during Ednyfed's time. In due course he survived his master to become lieutenant to his successor, Dafydd, dying in 1246. He was buried at Llandrillo, where the present church was originally his private chapel, but the tombstone bearing his name poses a problem. It says he was 'quodam vicarius', normally translated as 'a former vicar' ('quodam' being a mistake for 'quondam'). There was indeed a fifteenth century vicar called Ednyfed, but on the other hand 'vicar' is not necessarily to be taken in its present common ecclesiastical sense. It could mean that he was the prince's deputy or representative, a meaning also shared by 'lieutenant'. Ednyfed's descendants form one route from the Welsh dynasties to the Tudors.

Under the prince and his seneschal there was an elaborate hierarchy of administators. The 'maer' or mayor of each commote was replaced in power during this time by a new officer, the *rhaglaw*, lieutenant, the prince's representative. He was supported by a legal officer and by the steward of the *llys*, as the static courts were known. There was some administration involved, as each court had to be permanently provided for. Each *llys* in each commote was surrounded by demesne lands sufficient for its provision.

While all this stayed put, Llywelyn and the itinerant court moved from *llys* to *llys*. With him was his seneschal Ednyfed and also his chancellor, together with a small number of clerks. He was protected by the *teulu*, literally 'family', the familiar term for his household troops.

These courts were not far apart. From Trefriw to Conwy, or Conwy to Aber, is about eight miles. To go from Aber to Llanfaes you have to cross the Lafan Sands at low tide and then the narrow straight by ferry, but the distance is about the same. That there were major courts both at Rhosyr and Aberffraw, a few miles apart in western Anglesey, as has now become clear from the work done by the Gwynedd Archaeological Trust, perhaps indicates that they were not all in use at the same time. Since we know that Llywelyn occupied Aberffraw, and also that he issued a charter from Rhosyr in 1237, we must suppose that one of these clearly alternative sites was coming into use, the other going out, during his lifetime. Certainly most of the finds at Rhosyr indicate a slightly later date, the time of his son Dafydd and of the last Llywelyn. Courts at Caernarfon and Nefyn, on the Llyn peninsula, completed this chain.

Aberffraw had always been one of the principal seats of the kings of Gwynedd. There is nothing to be seen of the court there now, only a barely distinguishable bank in a field. It was widely assumed until the substantial stone wall-bases were uncovered in the early 1990s at Rhosyr that the reason for the disappearance of all Llywelyn's courts was that they were made of wood. It is known, certainly, that the court at Aberffraw was intentionally demolished and its timbers taken to repair and complete Caernarfon castle in 1317.

We know of Llywelyn's involvement in

the ancient seat of his ancestors at Aberffraw because he incorporated it in his title. Until the spring of 1230 he was known as 'Princeps Norwallie', that area in fact meaning Gwynedd. After that he became 'Princeps Aberffraw et dominus de Snowdon'.

Of the other *llysau*, the settlement at Trefriw, in the Conwy valley, is often referred to as a hunting-lodge, but since Llywelyn apparently preferred it to Aber we must suppose that some administration was carried on from there. It is said that when he was there he and his wife had to walk up the steep hill to the old church of Llanrhychwyn to the Sunday services, until he decied to found a church in the valley at Trefriw to save his wife the walk. Llanrhychwyn then was a larger settlement than Trefriw, a world of upland farms, and the old church already old when Llywelyn knew it.

Also with religious connections was his court at Conwy, being just outside the Cistercian abbey which he had helped to establish. Early records suggest that this was a mainly timber-built edifice which Edward I incorporated into his town wall, rebuildng its outer wall in stone – yet some of it must have been stone-built already,

since three large windows of it remain, with the result that Conwy wall has, perhaps uniquely, windows on its outside at this point.

At Aber, along the coast, there has been some dispute as to the location of the *llys*. It is often supposed, following Leland, that the motte known as Pen y Mwd formed the site, since he says that some of the builiding still stood there in his time, in the first half of the sixteenth century. However archaeological digs near the motte in the 1990s and in 2010 to 11 have revealed, as at Rhosyr, the bases of substantial stone buildings, which, although perhaps slightly later than Llywelyn's lifetime, may be an indication of where his court had been.

Llywelyn's courts were civil settlements and in their often lightly built form scarcely defendable. However they were supported by a network of impressive stone-buiilt and presumably permanently garrisoned castles. These lay at stategic points in relation to the court and to the borders of the kingdom. The ancient Gwynedd fortress at Deganwy, for instance, could send help if need be to the courts of Trefriw, Conwy and Aber. Its existence added security to the prince's passage between those places.

Llywelyn's castle-building belongs mainly to the 1220s, following the political consolidation of his rule. The castles guarded the main valley approaches to the heartland of Gwynedd. That at Ewloe ptotects the entry to Gwynedd via the coastal plain; Cricieth and Deganwy bracket the kingdom's coast; Dolwyddelan and Dolbadarn overlook main passes into the mountains; Castell y Bere, further south, overlooks the entry to Gwynedd from that direction up the winding Dysynni valley.

Among all these there is an interesting variation of style. Richard Avent, in his useful booklet *Castles of the Princes of Gwynedd* (HMSO, Cardiff, 1983) points out that castle-building at the time was undergoing an innovation. Until the turn of the 12th to 13th centuries keeps were square. So Dolwyddelan (where Llywelyn almost certainly replaced an earlier motte with the basis of the present building) has a square keep. But it must have been becoming apparent that a rounded form was easier to defend. Hence a transition takes place. The towers of Ewloe and Cricieth are of a D form, their rounded ends looking remarkably like Edward I's later wall-towers. Then, towards the end of the 1220s or in the 1230s, he built Dolbadarn castle, on the Nant Gwynant pass, and the tower is firmly round. Llywelyn had observed, it is thought, the changes taking place in the Norman castles along the English border.

King John died on 19th October, 1216, after a period of civil war between the king and the barons, during which (at the rebels' invitation) Louis, prince of France, had invaded to claim the English throne. John had been distracted from the threat from Wales by the civil war, and in October he became ill with dysentery. The new king, Henry III, John's eldest son, was only nine, and William Marshal, Earl of Pembroke, was appointed Regent. This was not a propitious situation for Llywelyn, since the two were long-standing rivals. His dilemma was resolved, however, when the English barons chose a course of appeasement and required his doing homage to Henry. This was no problem for Llywelyn, of course, since the king was his wife's half-brother. He was given safe-conduct to do homage at Worcester, in

1. *Castell y Bere*; 2. *Ewloe castle*; 3. *Dolbadarn castle*

1218, where it was agreed that he should keep the lands he had conquered and control of the royal castles of Cardigan and Carmarthen. Those in England who wished to see the young king made secure, and who feared the consequences if anarchy returned, seem to have recognised that Llywelyn's powerful support was needed at this time.

When William Marshal died in 1231 his son, the new Earl of Pembroke, opposed the king. Llywelyn sided with him in the quarrel. A state of war existed on the border for two years, before Henry (who suffered from his father's lack of funds and dependence on often hostile barons) decided to make peace, which he did at Middle in Shropshire, a place half-way between Shrewsbury and Ellesmere. The Peace of Middle set an initial truce for two years, but this was to be renewed from year to year, and the effect lasted for the rest of Llywelyn's reign. This gave to Wales a confidence in the future which it had previously lacked, and its capable ruler set about trying to make sure that this would continue.

Cistercian abbeys of the Welsh princes: 1.Valle Crucis; 2. Strata Florida; 3. Cymer

In the course of the campaign building up to this Llywelyn had taken a significant prisoner, in 1228: William de Braose, head at the time of the powerful and ancient de Braose family.[4] Following the tradition of the time of using marriage as a tool of diplomacy, it was arranged that William's daughter should marry Llywelyn's son, Dafydd. Alliance between the families would be greatly to the benefit of both, since the de Braose family formed one of the major Marcher lordships.

William came back, probably to arrange this, the year after his release, for the Easter of 1230. It was then that an event happened in Llywelyn's private life which reveals a side of him normally hidden from history. 'That year,' says the *Brut*, 'William Breos the Younger was hanged by Llywelyn ap Iorwerth, after he had been caught in the prince's chamber with king John's daughter, the prince's wife.'

Llywelyn then displays a very reasonable explosion of anger. He threw both parties into prison, and three days later hanged William in public in daytime outside his court at Crogen, near Bala. 'It was,' says Sir John Lloyd, 'the outraged husband, not the astute politician, who hanged William de Breos.'

What is more surprising to us is that the marriage then went ahead. Llywelyn wrote to the widow saying that the judgement had been given by his magnates, outraged by William's behaviour. But the letter expresses no regret, and of course the prince could have overruled the judgement. He adds that he hopes the marriage will go ahead, and that his friendship with the family will continue. It is, to us, an astonishing approach to the widow of someone you have just hanged. We might alternatively see it as a sign of geat magnanimity, since William had been guilty of disloyalty, or at the best assesment extreme folly.

But what of Joan? It takes two, after all, to instigate an infidelity. It seems that the prince's love for her was great enough to overcome his bitterness. She stayed in prison for a year, but in 1231 she was released and became again Llywelyn's valued mediator with the English Crown.

The Treaty of Worcester and then the Peace of Middle, referred to above, left Llywelyn in no doubt about his security in Wales. Perhaps mindful of the setback in Gwynedd caused by his grandfather's failure to establish an agreed successor, he set about trying to persuade his fellow princes in Wales to pronounce his son Dafydd to be his rightful heir. There was in fact the possibility of doubt, since Dafydd was the eldest son by his wife Joan, but this was not his first liaison. He had a former son, Gruffudd, by an early mistress, and Welsh law up to then would have recognised him, though illegitimate, to be the rightful heir. Changing the Welsh legal custom Llywelyn followed the example of the Lord Rhys, who had ensured that his legitimate son Gruffudd would be his heir, though there was an older illegitimate son who would have expected to inherit. We have seen that he himself, Llywelyn, had been recognised as the heir to Gwynedd because of being the offspring of a church-sanctioned marriage, but ironically because Dafydd himself died without issue the succession in due course ran through his half-brother Gruffudd's line.

Llywelyn took what measures he could to ensure agreement to his choice of the change in custom to favour Dafydd. In 1238 he called a council at the abbey of Strata Florida where he succeeded in persuading the Welsh chieftains to swear their loyalty to Dafydd. He had earlier strengthened the latter's position, in 1222, by obtaining the Pope's formal approval of his decision to change the law, and further in 1226 his Holiness's declaration that Dafydd's mother Joan was the legitimate daughter of King John.

The unfortunate Gruffudd had in the meantime been systematically sidelined. Gruffudd had the rule of Meirionnydd, but following complaints of his ruling of it Llywelyn had him removed from there, and although he was rehabilitated enough to lead an army for his father into south Wales in 1223, by 1228 he was out of favour again (probably because of the decision to install Dafydd as heir) and spent the next six years imprisoned in the ancestral castle of Deganwy.

During a life which (at least until the Peace of Middle) had been a constant engagement with military threats, within as well as adjoining Wales, Llywelyn had found time to foster and promote the monastic movement in Wales. This was chiefly centred on the great abbey of Strata Florida, itself, founded by the Lord Rhys, an offshoot of the Cistercian abbey of Whitland. From Strata Florida the Cistercians expanded further into Wales, to Cymer, near Dolgellau, where in 1209 Llywelyn gave them mining rights, and Penmon in Anglesey, which became Augustinian (with a more formal and structured regime which Llywelyn encouraged of the movement) which he enriched by the grant of lands. To the Abbey of Aberconwy, at Conwy, he granted a Charter, in which he gave the monks extensive lands and privileges, which made it one of the foremost religious houses in Wales. The dating of this event is anomalous, since it itself says it is 'given at Aberconwy in the year from the incarnation of our Lord one thousand one hundred and ninety-eight', and adds 'and in the tenth year of my princeship'. When did Llywelyn succeed to the princeship of Gwynedd? There is no single answer, since the process was gradual, but it cannot be thought to be before the late 1190s. He may, as Gerald says, have begun to exercise his influence in Gwynedd at a tender age 'during the period of our journey' (1188), but could not be said to have succeeded to princedom until he defeated his uncle Dafydd in 1194, or expelled him in 1197; or perhaps even until the defeat of Gruffudd in 1199, or the latter's death in 1200. That, in fact, would be a suitable date for the granting of a Charter to Aberconwy abbey, since Gruffudd died there.

Llywelyn's personal feelings were to

erupt again in 1237. He and his wife Joan were at his court in Aber when she died, court of the commote of Arllechwedd Uchaf, a favourite place of his.[5] She died on 2nd February. He had the body taken across the Lafan Sands and ferried to Llanfaes, in Anglesey, his nearest other court. There he had Bishop Hugh of St Asaph (the see of Bangor being at that time vacant) consecrate a burial ground. He set up there a house of Fransiscans, considered to be the holiest of monks, whose task was for ever to pray for her soul.

This they did until the Dissolution of the Monasteries.

The *llys* of Llanfaes had already gone by then, moved by Edward I to Newborough on the other side of the island, a safe distance from his new town of Beaumaris. There is nothing to be seen of either *llys* or monastery now, only a reference to the latter in the form of the name of a house: The Friars, which stands on part of the site. At the Dissolution the elaborately carved stone coffin which bore the Princess was rescued, and preserved for some centuries at Baron Hill, seat of the local landowning family. There after a bit people seem to have forgotten what it was, since it became a horse-trough. It was again rescued in 1808 and placed in the porch of Beaumaris church, where it still is.

In the year of Joan's death, or early the next one, Llywelyn, in his mid-60s, suffered a slight stroke. There was no change of policy in Gwynedd, and he remained its head, but from then on his son Dafydd took on the actual running of the country. Charters began to be issued in Dafydd's name, in 1238, the year in which the gathering of Welsh princes at Strata Florida had sworn allegiance to him. Dafydd began immediately to assert his power. He confiscated most of the territory held by his half-brother Gruffudd, and the next year went further by imprisoning him and his son Owain in Cricieth castle. It was not until after his father's death, when he suffered a defeat at the hands of his uncle the king of England, that he was obliged to release them. The unfortunate Gruffudd then became an English hostage (for the second time in his life), being now held in the Tower of London. True to his luck he died trying to escape, when the rope of sheets with which he was climbing out of the Tower proved too weak. He fell to his death, in March 1244.

When it became clear to them that Llywelyn was dying, his people hurried him to the Abbey of Aberconwy, where he was enrolled as a monk, and he died, as had his cousin Guffydd ap Cynan, wearing the simple robe of undyed wool which gave the 'white monks' their name, in the Abbey of Aberconwy, on 11th April 1240.

There he was buried, in the Abbey church. A little more than forty years later the world changed again, and when Edward I moved the whole monastery to Maenan, in the Conwy valley, the stone sarcophagus containing the coffin of the prince went too. It is not known where (or if) he was reburied, and all that remains (as in the case of Joan, his wife) is the big stone base of the outer coffin, which lies in the Wynn chapel adjoining the old church in Llanrwst.

NOTES

1. *Tempus Publishing, 2005. P. 108. Moore makes a valiant attempt to summarise the chaotic sequences referred to above.*

2. **Roger Turvey,** *Twenty-one Welsh Princes, Gwasg Carreg Gwalch, 2010. p. 89*

3. **Hostages.** *The Peniarth version of the Brut says the hostages were 'from among the leading men of the land', the Hergest version 'from amongst the gentlefolk' (o vonedhigyon). But neither mention the inclusion of Llywelyn's son. That he was one of the hostages is evidenced by no less an authority than Magna Carta. The fact that that document restored the hostages to Llywelyn shows that some remained after twenty-eight of them were hanged by John at Nottingham in 1212, in what is sometimes given as an instance of his temper.*

4. **De Braose.** *The name is spelt in many different ways, but derives from the town of Briouze, in Normandy, original home of the family. They came with William the Conqueror and received the barony of Bramber, Sussex, from where they spread to possess lands in the Welsh Marches at Builth and Radnor and later other border territories. Brewys in Welsh.*

5. **Aber.** *Whenever the place is named in the Welsh chronicles the name of it is 'Aber':* bu varw Dam Siwan verch Ieuan vrenhin... yn llys Aber, *and so on. Our historical sources, Leland, Pennant, Byng, Fenton, all knew it by that name. In modern times the historians Bezant Lowe, the Royal Commission on Ancient Monuments Inventory, Professor Dodd, H. R. Davies, and John Davies all call it Aber. Whatever justification there may be for the recent imposition of the name Abergwyngregin, there is none in the historical sources.*

Llywelyn ap Gruffudd

Henry III was clearly not willing to extend to Dafydd, who had succeeded his father as prince of Gwynedd and overall leader of the Welsh, the same powers as his father King John had allowed to Llywelyn Fawr. By demanding that he hand over his half-brother Gruffudd, and then imprisoning the latter himself, he revealed his intention of dividing Gwynedd. Gruffudd's death obstructed this, and Henry turned on Dafydd in more explicit ways. He invaded Gwynedd in 1241, when he achieved the transfer of Gruffudd, and launched a more serious invasion in 1245. A large force drawn from both England and Ireland followed the traditional route from Chester to Rhuddlan, and ended up in Deganwy. There they confronted the Conwy river and the limits of their power, since before long they (like the army of the king's father) began to run out of supplies. They were inadequately clothed and living in tents. The chronicler Matthew Paris quotes at length a letter written by a soldier in the king's army to a friend in England, in September 1245: 'We are oppressed by cold and nakedness, because our houses are of canvas and we are without winter clothing.' Food and wine was running out, and when a ship bringing provisions from Ireland entered the river it ran aground and was attacked by the Welsh. A battle ensued in which both sides displayed much bitterness and savagery.

The next year, the *Brut* tells us, 'was a rainy year'. In February Dafydd died, unexpectedly and from an unknown cause, in his court at Aber, as his mother had done, and was buried at Aberconwy Abbey. He was in his late thirties. He had no offspring.

Llywelyn's plan of ensuring the succession had not worked out, nor had the schemes of Henry for fragmenting Gwynedd. Gwynedd, it was agreed, would now be ruled by the sons of Gruffudd, Owain and his younger brother Llywelyn. These were the natural successors: grandsons of Llywelyn Fawr and nephews (so next of kin) to the previous ruler. The year after Dafydd's death they met, under Henry III's direction, at Woodstock, where agreement was reached for the share-out of territory. That the brothers had to arrange to meet, and under the auspices of

Rhuddlan castle

a neighbouring king, implies that they were not that close, and indeed their lives so far had been consistently separate. Llywelyn noticeably did not intervene when his father and brother were imprisoned by his uncle Dafydd and then by Henry. Perhaps in his adopting the position of natural heir to the childless Dafydd he had not anticipated the return of his elder brother from the Tower of London. At any rate it was not to be long before war developed, true to the traditions of their family, between the brothers.

The matter was complicated by the involvement of a younger brother, Dafydd, who also became something of a pawn to Henry in his continuing attempts to subdivide Gwynedd. Dafydd demanded a share of it, and was supported by his brother Owain and the English king. Llywelyn defeated his two brothers in 1255, and, now in sole command of Gwynedd, set about re-occupying the eastern extent of it, the Perfeddwlad, which had for some time been under the control of Henry. It had in fact been agreed as such by the Treaty of Woodstock, and Llywelyn's retaking of it amounted to breaching that

Denbigh castle in Perfeddwlad – the site of one of Dafydd's fortified courts

treaty. Henry's interference in the governance of Gwynedd, and the interests by the Crown in what had previously been the fiefdom of the Earl of Chester, signalled a new and threatening phase of diplomacy for Wales.

This movement towards central English involvement in Wales was considerably aggravated by the fact that Chester was no longer to be the private holding of a largely independent earl. When the earl John died childless in 1237 Henry kept the title and the territory in possession of the Crown. Having to be absent to deal with trouble in his continental realm in the 1250s he appointed his son Edward to rule England, and granted him the annexed earldom in 1254. With it went a claim to govern the rich part of Gwynedd between the Conwy and Chester, the Perfeddwlad; as far, that is, as the much-disputed castle of Deganwy.

A year after that, Edward, son of king Henry, he then being earl of Chester, came to survey his lands and his castles in Gwynedd round about August.

That is, in 1256. So says the Peniarth version of the Welsh chronicles. So it was that the future Edward I came to look across the Conwy river for the first time to the hostile bank ruled by Prince Llywelyn. The stage was set for the confrontation between the two, and events then moved irresistably towards it.

Edward went home to England shortly after that, but he had already gone too far, too soon. Given a free hand by his father, and then aged seventeen, he had imposed on the part of Wales under his power the sort of iron rule for which he would in due course become justifiably famous. He had done so, however, without taking account of the pride and resilience of its inhabitants. These, the princes and gentlefolk of Wales, came to Llywelyn in tears to complain that they had been deprived of liberty and property by the Saxons, 'and they made known to him that they peferred to be slain in war for their liberty than to suffer themselves to be unrighteously trampled upon by foreigners'. Llywelyn, we are told, was moved when he saw the tears of the high-born, and 'at their instigation and by their counsel and at their request' (in other words, I think, assured of widespread support) he moved into the Perfeddwlad and pressed on then into much of the rest of Wales.

By 1258 Llywelyn had started to style himself Prince of Wales, but there was still in this an element of wishful thinking. Dissent arose not so much from the English neighbours (occupied, as we shall see, with their own problems) but from closer at hand, particularly within his own family. His younger brother Dafydd, defeated along with his older brother Owain and for a time imprisoned by Llywelyn, had been released and enrolled as a partner in the assault on the border lands. But in 1263 Dafydd defected to the English. It will become apparent later in this story that there is much that we do not understand about Dafydd, but the basis of his behaviour may lie in an early resentment at not being assigned his own share of Gwynedd.

After some turbulent times along the border ('...at that time Edward, son of king Henry, came and burned some of the towns in Gwynedd') we suddenly find a period of calm:

In that year Wales had peace from the English, and Llywelyn ap Gruffudd was prince over all Wales.

1264: it was the year of the Battle of Lewes. The extent of internal trouble in Wales might lead us to assume England to be stable, but this was still far from being the case. The difficulties which King John had experienced were not yet over. Simon de Montfort was born and brought up in France, from a distinguished landowning family with hereditary claims to lands in both countries. He came to England in 1229, in his early twenties, and was welcomed at the court of Henry III, where French was the language spoken. His family's English inheritance was the earldom of Leicester, which had been annexed by King John in 1207, and although he was the third son one elder brother died in 1220 and he and the other brother came to an arrangement by which Simon would waive his rights in France and Amaury those in England, so that he had a claim to the Leicester inheritance. In 1238 he married Henry's sister Eleanor, and in 1239 the king restored him to the earldom. He was sufficiently in favour at the English court to be one of the godfathers to the royal heir, Edward. However as early as 1239 he and Henry fell out over an apparently trivial matter, de Montfort having named Henry without consent as the guarantor of a debt. In the meantime the dispute with the barons was far from resolved. It reached some sort of compromise in 1258, when an assembly was held in Oxford, where an army was assembling to launch a new attack into Wales. The country was in a state of famine, following a failed harvest the year before, and (the chronicler Matthew Paris says) poor people were dying of starvation.

There the king was obliged (as his father had been) to sign away some of his power. The 'Oxford Provisions' gave much of the control of the country to a standing committee, like a parliament. This sounded as if it would avoid further strife, but the king, like his father, chose to ignore the agreement. Civil War in England resulted, the 'Second Barons' War', culminating in the Battle of Lewes. This resulted in the virtual imprisonment of both the king and his son Edward, and it was only when the latter managed to escape to freedom that matters changed again. De Monfort was losing popularity when confronted by Edward's army at Evesham, in 1265.

In the meantime Llywelyn had been doing business with the rebels. It seems likely that his overall aim was to be recognised as rightful ruler of Wales, which the assumed title Prince of Wales implies, and since he must have known that the king, in his vulnerable position, would hesitate to have a kingdom on his border which he could not control, and that he would be supported in this stance by the Marcher Lords, who had reason to obstruct Llywelyn, he turned to the main body of barons under de Montfort, and, it seems, with some success. He underpinned his alliance with de Montfort by agreeing to marry the latter's daughter. This event, we shall see, was delayed by circumstances, but in the end it formed something of a milestone.

The new phase of the complex game was ratified by the Treaty of Pipton (in the Wye valley), in 1265. De Montfort was then virtually in control of the country, having Herny III and his son in custody, and it must have seemed to Llywelyn, not being able to see round the corner, that his aims had all been achieved. The Treaty gave him power over the Welsh princes, control of the central Marches, the hopes of future expansion, and it recognised his right to the title of Prince of Wales. That was on 19th June. On 28th May Edward had escaped from de Montfort's custody, not far away, at Hereford. Presumably both parties knew this, at Pipton. It may be that they also took into account the weakening of de Montfort's position by the royal

prince's freedom, and the wisdom, in the circumstances, of having the powerful Welsh prince on his side. The flowering of the new friendship lasted for a little while. But that same year, on 4th August, de Montfort died in a massacre by Edward's forces at Evesham, and Llywelyn was not there to help him.

If we may summarise this brief period of extreme uncertainty in England and Wales, say 1258 to 1265, it can be seen that it was the perilous state of Henry III's crown that enabled Llywelyn to become unchallenged ruler of more of Wales and areas across its borders than any former leader. It was then to be Henry's son Edward who reversed both situations, restoring security to the throne of England and curtailing the ambitions of the ruler of Wales.

To begin with all went well for Llywelyn. It was, of course, just as well that he had not supported de Montfort at Evesham. In fact the ratification by Henry of the terms of Pipton in the form of the Treaty of Montgomery, in September 1267, was probably Llywelyn's peak of power. Henry's main concern was to restore the security of his crown, and baronial unrest continued to threaten this. At Montgomery it was agreed that the title

Prince of Wales would be recognised by the English as well as the Welsh leaders; his rights over the territories of other Welsh princes extended to the whole of Wales – that is, in modern terms, everything except the southern coastline states of Glamorgan, Gower, and Pembroke. Llywelyn was not content with this. He continued to put pressure on Glamorgan, the realm of Gilbert de Clare, causing de Clare to build Caerphilly castle to defend his lands.

Llywelyn destroyed de Clare's first castle, so he built a second one, in 1270. By this time Llywelyn's position must have seemed even stronger, not least because the English heir, the Lord Edward, was away. The prince set off on crusade in 1270, and it was to be four years before he returned. In the meantime, in his absence, he became king of England.

Before he left for the Holy Land Edward had been in charge of the purges which folowed the civil war. All barons who had supported de Montfort were to be disposessed (though this was diluted to being allowed to buy back their lands) – yet Llywelyn seems to have gone unscathed, and he, betrothed to de Montfort's daughter, could hardly avoid

attention. It must have been a deliberate policy on Edward's part to keep Wales powerful, but if so, this was not to last.

Edward's four years away were fruitful to him and to history, since they left him with European, or even global, ambitions. He had, from the start, a territorial interest in Gascony, then an English colony, which had been granted to him in 1249. Now from the Holy Land he left for Sicily, and he was there in 1272 when he received the news that his father had died and he had been proclaimed king. The fact that he did not feel the need to hurry home indicates a certain confidence of the security of his position. He then spent some time in Italy, visiting the Pope in Rome, and then in France, where he met the king in Paris and went to oversee his affairs in Gascony, staying to put down a minor rebellion, returning to England on 2nd August 1274. His coronation took place on August 19th.

One thing that Edward discovered on becoming king was how confident Llywelyn had become in Wales. Something which is evident to us now probably became clear to him then as well. It was that Llywelyn's success had to a large extent been gained at Edward's expense. It was his lands, given him by his father on the Cheshire border and in mid and south Wales, which Llywelyn had overrun. Edward found on his return that the prince of Wales had consistently been retreating from the terms of the Treaty of Montgomery, delaying his annual payments and overstepping the agreed bounds of his principality by (for instance) building a castle near Montgomery.

That year, 1274, was not a good one for Llywelyn. His brother Dafydd, who had defected to the English as long ago as 1263 and as part of the Treaty of Montgomery had been restored to his lands in Wales, now conspired with the leader of southern Powys to oust Llywelyn and take over the principality. Llywelyn moved against the traitors at once, but they fled to England where they were given royal protection.

The next year Edward came to Chester and summoned Llywelyn to him to do homage. It was a demand which was to have devastating consequences, and it would be hard to believe that both parties were not aware of the dilemma it posed. Because of its importance it is sometimes questioned why Llywelyn refused to go; but the matter is quite clear, and is stated as such by the *Brut*. He 'did not go to the king because he was maintaining his foes, namely Dafydd

ap Gruffudd, his brother, and Gruffudd ap Gwenwynwyn.' (We have to remember that the feudal notion of homage was based on a contract by a superior power to protect the renderer of homage against his enemies). 'And for that reason the king returned enraged to England.'

yn llidyawc: angry, or enflamed. Edward was not a man used to being contradicted. He had a short temper, it is known, and this was much feared by those around him. That year, the chronicle tells us, there was (by coincidence?) an earthquake which was felt all over Wales.

In this particular case Edward showed remarkable patience. He actually sent for the prince three times more, each time with the response of a stubborn refusal. The last time, in April 1276, would have seemed to have been final, but even then Edward attempted to negociate. He sent the archbishop of Canterbury to Wales as his emissary, and Llywelyn duly explained his terms. He would not risk going to London, possibly bearing in mind that his father, Gruffudd, had ended his days in the

The Treaty of Montgomery was signed at Rhydchwima (the ford of Rhydwhyman) on the Severn

1

2

3

Tower. Instead he would do homage at Oswestry or Montgomery, but only after his wrongs had been put right. But for Edward on his part Llywelyn's submission had to be unconditional.

It certainly seems as if both sides were aware of the dangers of the situation. For 1276 the chronicle says: 'Llywelyn sent messengers frequently to the king's court to seek to arrange peace between them. But that was of no avail.'

We feel now, of course, that a little less relentlessness on either side would have done the trick; but here we are not dealing with relenting men. Their respective positions must have seemed to each of them highly reasonable. To Edward, Llywelyn had broken the Treaty of Montgomery by refusing to do him homage. To Llywelyn it was too much to ask that he go to do homage at a court where his enemies were honoured guests.

A further complication was the question of Llywelyn's marriage. His wife-to-be, de Montfort's daughter, had been taken to France for her own safety, and the

Norman strongholds: 1. Another army leaving Chester to attack Wales; 2. Montgomery; 3. Oswestry castle

marriage had been undertaken by proxy. Edward cannot have viewed it as anything other than provocation. De Montfort was the enemy of his family, the force which had endangered the Crown. To contemplate the same threat rekindling now in Wales must have seemed to him unthinkable. It was probably not by coincidence that when the princess sailed to join her husband, in 1275, the ship was boarded in the Bristol Channel and she was taken to Windsor. This of course rendered it all the more impossible for Llywelyn to do homage on Edward's terms.

Eleanor was released from Windsor after intervention by the Pope, and in due course she and Llywelyn solemnised their marriage. The chronicles have this taking place twice, so we assume some error of copying: in Winchester, in 1275, and in Worcester in 1278.

Things reached a point of no-return in November, 1276, when Edward declared Llywelyn to be a rebel, and assembled an army at Worcester to undertake a three-pronged attack on Wales. In effect the war started the next January, with the garrisoning of castles in the Marches. Edward operated a system of local recruitment which relied on growing discontentment with Llywelyn's power. When, by that summer, his army reached a total of 15,640 men, some 9000 of those were Welsh.

Edward came to Chester to deal directly with the matter of removing the prince, in June. It is clear that he had a detailed plan in place. In Chester he was supported by a fleet, and prepared, with this, a pincer movement along the Welsh coast. He had foresters and road-makers in his army, just as he had every other sort of expert. A great swathe was cut through the forests of the western Cheshrie plain as the huge force advanced.

It was plain that this time they intended to stay. In July Edward started to build a castle at Flint. This was to be hisheadquarters while work was taking place to expand the old Norman fortress at Rhuddlan. In August he was at Deganwy, where the castle was still unrepaired after Llywelyn's destruction of it, so that the king and the army must have camped on the hill below it. It was there, in August 1277, that he took the fateful decision not to rebuild Deganwy, but to build instead a fortress defending the far, not the near, side of the river crossing.

Maybe this had been his ambition for some time, and it certainly made sense in terms of military strategy. Without control of the western bank he could not command the river, and his supply ships, as he knew from his father's experience, entered it at risk. With a castle on the further bank he could not only dominate the land and sea routes, the harbour and the river crossing, but could strike from that base into the heartland of Snowdonia.

Several things had to take place before that was possible. Edward's effective military tactics pressed ahead in the meantime. First, he made use of his fleet to destroy the Welsh food supply. Now that the Cheshire plain was in English hands the principality relied for flour on the grain crops of Anglesey, and in August these were growing ripe. The fleet landed in Anglesey during the first two weeks of September, and the grain was harvested by three hundred and sixty reapers working for the English Crown.

This was a blow which Llywelyn could not sustain. He came to Edward at Rhuddlan and offered to submit, and a treaty was signed at the Abbey of Aberconwy, on 9th November, 1277.

Flint castle

It is at first glance hard to see why Edward should agree to terms at all. He could have simply proceeded to occupy Wales, as he eventually did. By November 1277 however two factors combined to make him cautious: winter was setting in, and he knew the danger of campaigning in Wales in bad weather. Secondly, the war was getting expensive. Edward's economy is a subject in itself; he borrowed, for instance, from Italian bankers. He knew however how dangerous it was for a king to be in debt, and his father's and grandfather's experience of trying to recover from that state by raising taxes had not been propitious. By the time he had completed his great programme of castle-building he would be effectively bankrupt, but for the moment he seems to have hoped for another way forward.

The Treaty of Aberconwy allowed Llywelyn to retain the title of Prince of Wales, but the rest of the content of the treaty made it clear that this was now little more than a pretence. The other claimants to territories in Wales were now to rule them independently of him: he was to be no longer their overlord. He, Llywelyn, now ruled as sovereign lord only over the inner heartland of Gwynedd, the part beyond the Conwy, without the Perfeddwlad, part of which was granted to Dafydd (though subject still to the overerlordship of Edward), and in Anglesey only as vassal to the king. The matter was therefore left with the potential for further disputes, which arose particularly through the type of law which was to be enforced, whether English or Welsh, in each individual case.

In the immediate aftermath of the settlement of the peace some surprising things took place. When the two antagonists met to seal it, in November 1277, Edward invited Llywelyn to spend Christmas with him in London. Perhaps it was more of an order than a suggestion, but for whatever reason Llywelyn (who had caused the war by refusing to go to London) went, and spent two weeks at court in Westminster. There he did the act of homage which he had so adamantly refused. They met again when Edward came to Rhuddlan in 1278 to supervise the work in progress there, and all the signs are that his was the cementing of a new friendship. The next month Edward went to extraordinary lengths to display this. He and his brother Edmund presented Llywelyn with his bride, Eleanor, who was in any case their cousin, waiting for him at the door of Worcester cathedral, 'at the door of the great church at Worcester'. They went through a formal wedding service (again?) and a banquet was held that night, for which the king paid. 'And on the following day Llywelyn and Eleanor returned joyfully to Wales.'

Everything, it might then have seemed, was to turn out for the good. The attempt to thwart the marriage had been reversed, as had the refusal of homage. But back home there was still much dissatisfaction.

Dafydd in particular was left discontented. He clearly felt that by defecting to the English Crown he had deserved a securer status in Wales. Instead he found that he and his subjects were mistreated by crown officials and the new colonists of Edward's boroughs, such as the recently founded town of Rhuddlan. Both brothers suffered the unsatisfactory conditions of the Treaty for several years, but they now had a common cause for resistance, and when in March 1282, on Palm Sunday, Dafydd led an attack on Hawarden Castle (one of the royal castles of the Marches, in the area of his supposed territory) Llywelyn was under pressure to provide support. The revolt spread quickly during March, reaching into mid Wales; but still Llywelyn hesitated. It was clear to him of course that he had much to lose either way: if Dafydd was successful he could take Llywelyn's place as Welsh leader; if he failed it would be as well not to fail with him.

It is often suggested that a personal loss triggered his fateful decision. The dating supports this, and it is not to be supposed that Llywelyn ap Grufydd was any less human than his eminent grandfather. On 19th June his wife died in childbirth, giving birth to their only child, Gwenllian. Like the beloved wife of Llywelyn Fawr and like their son and successor Dafydd she died at the old Gwynedd court of Aber, and she too was buried at the Abbey of Aberconwy. Whether as a reaction to this blow, or for some other reason, Llywelyn then joined the war.

The difference between the two brothers is significant to history, and Dafydd's persistent bitterness was to be fatal to them both. If the matter had been left to Edward and Llywelyn the peace achieved by the Treaty of Aberconwy could have survived. Edward, though taken by surprise, reacted with typical

determination to the Palm Sunday attack. By July his fleet was in the Dee estuary again, and he himself was in Chester, where the army was mustering. By the autumn of 1282 the king's fleet and army had taken Anglesey, and an attempt was made to invade Snowdonia from there. Llywelyn himself was at his court at Aber, when an event of some farcical absurdity took place on the Menai Strait.

A bridge of boats had been built to convey the army, now in Anglesey, to the mainland. It seems that its weight-bearing capacity had been finely judged, allowing the troops to cross it in single file. When the ones in front reached the point at which they could see the enemy bank they became aware that the Welsh were waiting for them, and started turning back. The doubling of the weight on the boat-bridge caused it to collapse, and a large part of the army (encumbered by full armour) drowned.[1]

At the same time the Archbishop of Canterbury had been sent to Llywelyn at Aber to talk terms. This however only had a slight delaying effect on the course of the war. The Archbishop shuttled backward

1. *Archaelogical finds at Llywelyn's court at Abergwyngregyn; 2. Dolforwyn; 3. Hawarden*

and forward for a bit between Aber and Rhuddlan (which Edward had made his headquarters). But his efforts were in vain. The only terms which Edward offered, Llywelyn could not accept: it would involve giving up rule of Wales and going into exile, and Llywelyn replied that such demands had amazed him and his council. They would, he said, not have allowed him to consent to these terms even if he had wished to.

It was November by the time Llywelyn felt able to emerge from Gwynedd and set off in search of help from other parts of Wales: from Powys, Builth, Brecon. He had left the dubious Dafydd in charge of the security of Snowdonia, to where he expected to return to sit out a winter confrontation. But something had happened in the meantime, which unfortunately is tantalisingly unexplained.

'And at that time', runs the *Brenhinedd y Saesson* version of the chronicles, 'the betrayal of Llywelyn was effected in the belfries of Bangor by his own men'. We are told no more than that, but the inference must leave in our minds the suspicion that what then happened was not the accident of war which it is conventionally portrayed as, but the result of a conspiracy.

Llywelyn had got separated from the main part of his army, but this was apparently intentional. He had sent them ahead to confirm the support of Brecon. It seems that the king's army, though administered from Rhuddlan, knew where he was. 'And then Roger Mortimer and Gruffudd ap Gwenwynwyn, and with them the king's host, came without warning upon Llywelyn ap Gruffudd and slew him and many of his host...'

There are two other versions of exactly what happened, but they come from chroniclers in England and both date from some time after the event. In one, the attack was first directed against the main body of the Welsh army, from which the prince was separated. When he heard the noise of battle he was on the way to join it when he was struck down by a lancer, who did not know who he was.

The other has him being lured into a trap under the pretext of an offer of peace with the Mortimers and Gruffudd, then separated from his troops by a skirmish and chased into a wood, where he was cornered and slain.

Whatever the details, the outcome took place at the conflict known as the Battle of Orewin Bridge, on the banks of the river Irfon, in the area of Builth, on 11th December, 1282.

Llywelyn's head was struck off and taken to Edward at Rhuddlan. After displaying it to his troops in Anglesey the king had it sent to London, where it eventually set up over the gate of the Tower of London. Llywelyn's body was most probably taken for burial by the monks of the nearby Cistercian abbey of Cwm Hir, at Maelienydd. A fine monument now stands at Cilmeri, near Builth, at the supposed site of his death

NOTES

1. ***The bridge of boats.*** *Some records blame the tides for its failure, and indeed anyone who has sailed in the Menai Strait knows the complexity of their two-way flow. But a bridge of boats is an obviously fragile thing, not best suited to the passage of armoured soldiers.*

1. *Cilmeri memorial stone to Llywelyn;*
2. *site of Llywelyn's grave at Abbey Cwm Hir*

Aftermath

If Dafydd had been involved in a conspiracy to have his brother slain by the royal and Marcher troops near Builth, it did not of course pay off for him as he might have expected. There are faint reasons for supposing he might have done this, since he presumably knew where Llywelyn was and he himself, ensconced in the heartland of Gwynedd, was (at last) in a position to assert what he clearly felt were his rights to rule at least some of the principality. For a time, in any case, he attempted to carry on the war. His weakness was that he could not command the allegiance which the Welsh had given Llywelyn. Edward for his part did not attempt to tackle the heartland of Snowdonia from the wrong side of the Conwy. The most significant event of the last phase of the war was the fall of Dolwyddelan castle, on 18th January 1283, which enabled him to come down the Conwy valley on its western side, his men cutting their way through the ancient forest which still clothed its bank. That way he could arrive at the Cistercian monastery of Aberconwy, where (because of course he knew it well) he had probably already decided to found the castle and garrison town of Conwy.

It was an essential step towards the total blockade of inner Gwynedd, which Edward planned to surround with a ring of mutually supporting castle towns – Conwy, Caernarfon, Cricieth, Harlech and a little later Beaumaris. When he was in Savoy on his way home from crusade he had met a master-builder, known as Master James of St George, after the fortress town of St Georges de l'Esperanche, near Lyon, which he had constructed for the Count of Savoy. He was in the employment of Count Philip when Edward met him, and since the count was a cousin of his Edward had stayed with him, perhaps at the town itself, in 1273. Evidently he had been impressed by the 'bastide' towns then forming an innovation in those parts of France. Bastide is a term in the Occitan language spoken in the area (and probably also one

1. Conwy; 2. Cricieth;
3. Caernarfon

of the languages of Edward and Master James) meaning originally a place under construction, later coming to describe the many fortified towns, in the form of castle and town wall, then being built in southern France. Edward arranged with Philip of Savoy to have the castle-builder transferred into his service, and James came to England probably in 1278. The chronicles say that the main phase of castle-building in Wales began in 1283, and the king's son Edward was born in Caernarfon in April of the next year, so evidently the building programme progressed fast, and evidently also the king was there to supervise the work.

With Gwynedd effectively conquered Dafydd 'fled into outlawry to the wilderness', in fact to his grandfather's stronghold of Castell y Bere, a sprawling hilltop citadel overlooking the Dysynni valley between Barmouth and Towyn, where he held out for a few more months. The royal and Marcher forces closed in on him, and, still in April 1283, there were 3,600 men surrounding Castell y Bere. Dafydd's forces were too few to protect

Beaumaris – Edward's response to another Welsh revolt

Dafydd's memorial plaque at Shrewsbury

him, and his support in the surrounding countryside was also weak. When his fortress surrendered (on 25th April) he himself disappeared into the hills, where he was hunted down by his own people and captured on the slopes of Cader Idris, on 28th June.

Dafydd was for a time imprisoned at Rhuddlan, but later in the year taken to Shrewsbury, where he was tried for treason on 2nd October and (hardly surpisingly) found guilty. He was dragged through the streets of Shrewsbury, hanged and then beheaded, finally quartered and disembowelled. His head was taken to London and displayed next to his brother's at the Tower.

The Treaty of Aberconwy had effectively commandeered to Edward much of Wales, but there remained the question of the inheritance of what was left. With no male heirs to inherit inner Gwynedd, Edward's attention turned to Llywelyn's only child, his daughter Gwenllian. To guard against her marrying and producing a future claimant Edward had the child taken to England and subsequently made to become a nun. The title of Prince of Wales he retained for the English Crown, and in due course bestowed it on his son, Edward of Caernarfon, when he became seventeen. It has ever since been the custom for the monarch to give the title to his or her eldest son.[1]

Edward celebrated his conquest of Gwynedd, and probably also the birth of his son, with a tournament and (with an appropriate reference) an Arthurian Round Table, in July, in the depths of its heartland, at the old court of Nefyn on the Llŷn peninsula, Then (says the Welsh chronicler) 'the king went happily jubilant to England, having conquered for himself all Gwynedd'. He had, however, done some business before he went.

In March of that eventful year, 1284, Edward had called a Parliament at Rhuddlan, where a plaque still marks the spot of his Parliament Building, though giving the date for its calling as 1283. The plaque is also wrong about the purpose of the meeting: 'securing to the principality of Wales its judicial rights and independence.' The Statute of Rhuddlan did not set out to be so benign.

Still findng fault with this unfortunate inscription we should note that the famous Statute was not strictly speaking a Statute at all. It was a royal proclamation, and did not pass through Parliament, even if Edward did call one in Rhuddlan town. It thus issued from Rhuddlan castle, where the king was ensconced, rather than from the Parliament Building. The preamble to it makes its intention clear. Divine Providence

1. Gwenllian's memorial, Sempringham;
2. Rhuddlan parliament house;
3. Detail of Rhuddlan's plaque

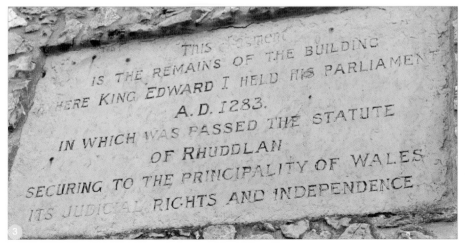

THIS monument
IS THE REMAINS OF THE BUILDING
IN WHERE KING EDWARD I HELD HIS PARLIAMENT
A.D. 1283.
IN WHICH WAS PASSED THE STATUTE
OF RHUDDLAN
SECURING TO THE PRINCIPALITY OF WALES
ITS JUDICIAL RIGHTS AND INDEPENDENCE

hath now of its favour wholly and entirely transferred under our proper dominion the land of Wales, with its inhabitants, heretofore subject unto us in feudal right, all obstacles whatsoever ceasing, and hath annexed and united the same unto the crown of the aforesaid realm, as a member of the same body.

To facilitate this domination the Statute set out to change the system of law, which in Wales was still that of the code developed from the lawbooks derived from Hywel Dda, and replace it with a mixture of adapted Welsh and imported English. The annexation of the whole country to the Crown of England was a feudal matter. Llywelyn had held it, as Edward would see it, as his vassal, and in rebelling had broken his part of the bargain. The land then reverted inevitably to the Crown. It would also have seemed proved to Edward that Divine Providence approved, since he had won the war as well by force of arms.

The main impositions which fell now on the previously free areas were those of the system of law, and of the apparatus of administration. The Norman shire system was imposed on Gwynedd, which had previously been divided into lordships. In these new shires crown officials (sheriffs and bailiffs) were now to control justice and order, and to collect taxes. Over the whole were two main officials, the Justiciar and the Chamberlain, both of whom operated from Caernarfon castle, which became effectively the capital of the new Crown land.

The words and terms of the Statute make clear that Edward thought of Wales now as a conquered country, 'wholly and entirely transferred under our proper dominion,' but this, it is plain, is not how Wales thought of itself. Over the course of some four hundred years (as we have just seen) Wales had developed from being the diverse residue of tribal kingdoms left from a pre-Roman Britain into something of a contemporary entity. A coherence had grown around it. It had become a nation, and you cannot simply legislate-away a nation.

In military terms of course he was right. He had won the war. He then set about showing that this gave him the power to impose control of other sorts,

Harlech castle – Edward secured a foothold on a rock on the edge of Snowdonia

legal and financial, on the conquered land. But one of several lessons the Statute of Rhuddlan teaches us is that such legislation (which does not attempt to take account of the values and aspirations of a people) does not lead to peace. There was war again in Wales within ten years.

Madog ap Llywelyn was the son of a disposesed lord of Meirionnydd, living in England. He returned to Wales, where discontent was swelling towards revolution. When rebellion erupted in 1294 he accepted the role of its leader, and although only distantly descended from the royal house of Aberffraw he assumed the title of Prince of Wales. The revolt seems to have been well co-ordinated, since it broke out all over Wales at the same time. Madog's rebel army challenged Edward's power successfully in northern Wales for a time in the winter of 1294 to 5. They overran the incomplete town walls of Caernarfon, took the town, hanged the king's officer, stormed into the castle over the foundations of its north walls, and burnt everything which would burn. A considerable amount of the building work would then have to begin again. When Edward came into Gwynedd he found himself at Christmas time in extreme danger besieged in Conwy castle, the town taken and burnt. Gwynedd and Anglesey were then in rebel hands. His baggage train had been ambushed and commandeered on the road back from Bangor, and he found the bulk of his army still on the wrong side of the Conwy, which was in flood. He postponed Christmas until the flood abated and supplies could reach him, in the meantime no doubt giving thanks for Conwy castle's strength. The rebellion collapsed when Madog led his forces into Powys and they were surprised and routed by the Earl of Warwick; he himself fled and later surrendered, disappearing from recorded history.

This was not the last instance of armed conflict on this issue of who rules Wales. The revolt under Owain Glyndŵr, in 1400, came much closer to success. It had the distinction too of not just being based on complaints of unfair taxes and high-handed officials, but, instead, the more positive aim of holding out the promise of independent Welsh institutions to serve and express an independent culture of Wales. This concept was founded on the

Owain Glyndŵr's rebellion is celebrated with his statue at Corwen

long and ancient process of development which we have been considering in this book, a slowly established bedrock of assumptions which proved to be at the same time both residual and seminal. It was built on heroism and ideals, and the Glyndŵr revolt in effect picked this up and magnified it. It then presented the image to the future as a prototype and a source of hope.

1. Site of Glyndŵr's famous victory at Bryn Glas, Pilleth; 2. Glyndŵr's Parliament House at Machynlleth; 3. The 'rebel's spirit' memorial to Llywelyn ap Gruffudd from Cayo, Glyndŵr's supporter at Llandovery

Glyndŵr's revolt lasted long enough to leave its permanent mark on the cultural history of Wales. Its leader presented himself as the most recent of the independent Princes, styling himself Prince of Wales, and in doing so formed a link, a bridge, between those paradigms and the emergence of the modern model of a Welsh nation state. But it too, like so many brave ideals before, was undepinned (and undermined) by the idea of right being proved by brute force rather than reasoning and persuasion, and sure enough it too failed in its immediate intention.

All this effort and anguish – the particular uprising itself and indeed the hopes of the hundreds of years before it – has not in the end been fruitless. By its occurrence it has served the valuable purpose of proposing an ideal, towards which the future would reliably work: the expression and celebration of Wales's latent identity, which has subsequently asserted itself in more peaceful ways.

The National Senedd – Wales's parliament – at Cardiff, established in 1997

NOTES

1. ***Prince of Wales.*** *In his Foreword to David Moore's book,* The Welsh Wars of Independence, *cited above, Lord (Dafydd) Elis-Thomas makes a brave and coherent suggestion that the time may come when Wales need no longer regard itself as a Principality, but now as having 'national equality within' the United Kingdom.*

Note: By way of ***Bibliography*** *for this chapter, three books may be recommended as being of value: The Oxford History of England volume* The Thirteenth Century, *by Sir Maurice Powicke, 1962;* The Welsh Wars of Independence *by David Moore (cited in a note above), Tempus Publishing Limited, 2005;* The Taming of the Dragon, Edward I and the Conquest of Wales, *by W. B. Bartlett, Sutton Publishing Limited, 2003.*